AF215916

Cap. I.

Juel del: Clemens Sculps.

DANISH LITERATURE

Saxo Grammaticus to Isak Dinesen

An exhibition at
the Houghton Library
October 16–November 21
by Nancy S. Reinhardt

1986

The Harvard College Library
Cambridge, Massachusetts

IDENTIFICATION OF UNCAPTIONED ILLUSTRATIONS

Copyright © 1986 by the President and Fellows of Harvard College

Design and production by Richard C. Bartlett and Deborah S. Davies
Photography by Victor Santamaria, Daniel Sullivan, and Rick Stafford.
Set in Bembo by Crane Typsetting Service, Inc.
Printed and bound by the Office of the University Publisher

Sponsors of the Exhibition

AMERICAN-SCANDINAVIAN FOUNDATION: DONALD F. HYDE
MEMORIAL FUND
CARLSBERG BEQUEST IN MEMORY OF BREWER J. C. JACOBSEN
DEN DANSKE BANK
EDWARD H. MICHELSEN
A. P. MØLLER & CHASTINE McKINNEY MØLLER'S FOUNDATION
NOVO INDUSTRIAS
HAVEN O'MORE
EGMONT H. PETERSENS FOND
THE QUEEN'S & PRINCE'S FOUNDATION

Preface

𝕿

"Such a collection of rare things as is not to be found under the Western star." Thus did the newly-appointed Smith Professor of Modern Languages, Henry Wadsworth Longfellow, describe in 1835 the books he was selecting for the Library during a season abroad, while he prepared himself for teaching. Among those "rare things" are six Danish books featured in this exhibition, proving the poet's acumen as a selector of books.

But a collection of rare things can be forgotten or overlooked if it is not increased and developed. By the end of the century the widow of Boston's Danish consul, Emil Christian Hammer, gave funds to buy Scandinavian books, and in 1904 Harvard's great collection builder Archibald Cary Coolidge gave some good Danish books. Two of the Hammer books and seven of the Coolidge books are shown here.

In 1965 the auction sale of Oscar and Lia Ekman's books at Branners Bibliofile Antiqvariat and Arne Bruun Rasmussen in Copenhagen encouraged Houghton's librarians to collect Scandinavian books actively, often advised by the antiquarian bookseller Hans Bagger. The George L. Lincoln fund and the Amy Lowell trust made possible the purchase of numerous rarities. In 1974 Mr. and Mrs. Robert D. Graff gave their splendid collection of Isak Dinesen, incorporating materials gathered by Dinesen's biographer and friend, Parmenia Ekstrom.

Even so, gaps remain, as our borrowing for this exhibition makes clear. We are grateful to David P. Wheatland for lending the crucial pamphlet of Ørsted, to Janet Jurist for lending one volume of the American letters of Wilhelm Dinesen, and to our colleague at the Boston Public Library, Laura Monti, for lending Nexø's rare first book.

The exhibition has encouraged several gifts. Harrison D. Horblit gave one of his greatest books, Tycho Brahe's *De stella nova* (1573), while the Friends of the Harvard College Library gave another first book, Hans Christian Andersen's. Our Keeper of Printed Books, James E. Walsh, a long-time acquisitor of Danica, has decided to present his own collection of Isak Dinesen, including things missed by the Graffs.

Many Danish friends, old and new, encouraged by the strength of Harvard's collection, have offered help to this project. Among them are the scholar Erik Dal, who recalled items he had discovered at Harvard; the artist Ole Hamann, who contributed the design of the poster; and Ambassador Eigil Jørgensen who encouraged support. Donors of funds, without whose generous sponsorship this catalogue could not have been printed, are listed above on page 5.

The exhibition, so ably constructed and annotated by Rare Books Cataloger Nancy S. Reinhardt, was inspired by our new Cambridge neighbor Mrs. Yoyo Tesdorpf Jones. To her, our tireless advisor and constant helper, we dedicate, in honor of her native literature, this special "collection of rare things."

Roger E. Stoddard
Curator of Rare Books

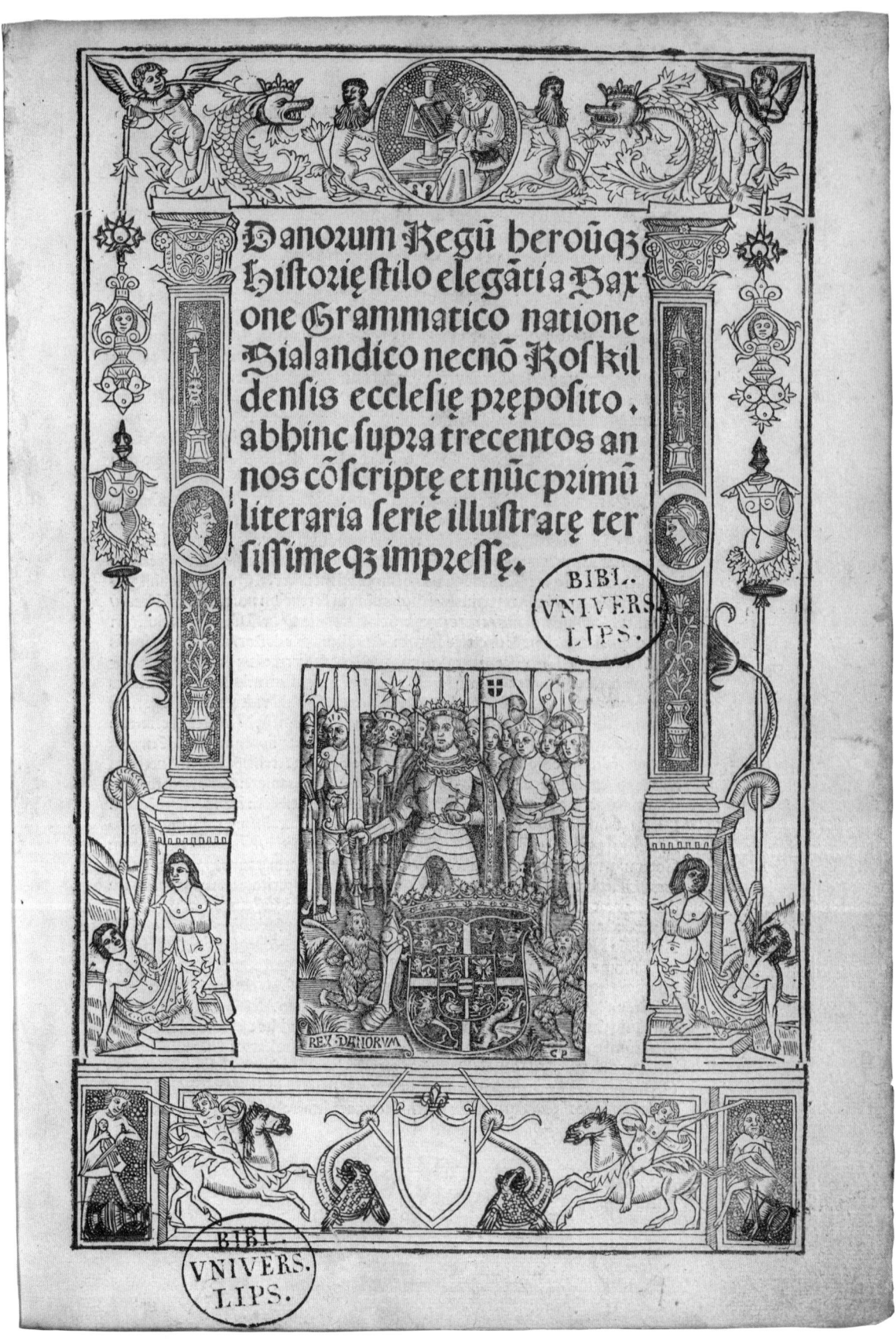

1 Saxo Grammaticus *Danorum Regu[m] Herou[m]q[ue] Historię* Paris, 1514

The Beginnings

The roots of Danish literature can be traced to the Bronze Age and the beginnings of Northern mythology. The earliest myths and legends were handed down from generation to generation by bards, the "singers of tales." It was much later, during the Age of the Vikings, that Scandinavian literature began to flower. In the ninth century, Harald Fairhair tried to unify the Norwegians under one rule, driving into exile the rebellious lords and "little kings" who refused to capitulate. Many traveled west and settled in Iceland. The civilization that emerged in these isolated regions produced brilliant and enduring texts which have influenced all of Scandinavian literature—the heroic sagas and the intricately patterned skaldic verses of Iceland. It was not until several centuries later, well after Christianity had been formally accepted in the North, that clerics, poets and historians put this rich oral tradition into writing. The only traces of earlier writing remaining from pre-Christian Scandinavia are the runic inscriptions found in Sweden, Norway and Denmark. Snorri Sturluson, Icelandic poet and historian of the thirteenth century, is one of the first and most famous of later Christian writers to recreate in his own words some of the early Icelandic tales. A number of these sagas were not written down until many years after Snorri, even as late as the fourteenth century.

The first Dane to gain recognition as poet and chronicler of early legends is Saxo Grammaticus, who composed what many consider the first significant work of Danish literature, the *Gesta Danorum*, a history of Danish kings (1). Were it not for the efforts of Christian Pedersen—who located, edited, and published the Saxo and other Danish manuscripts and then had them sent back to Denmark—many early Danish texts might have been lost to history. Pedersen also began a translation of Saxo's Latin into Danish, a task which Anders Sørensen Vedel completed in 1575. For his pioneering work, Pedersen is sometimes called "the father of Danish literature."

When Christian Pedersen returned via Holland to Denmark in the 1530s, he brought with him the spirit of the Reformation and the desire to publish reformed religious texts in the vernacular. It was mostly through his efforts that the first Bible was published in Danish (2).

The technology of printing also helped to spread the Reformation to the more remote regions of the Danish kingdom such as Iceland, which remained part of Denmark until 1944 when it was granted independent status. Gudbrand Thorlaksson, having been appointed bishop in Iceland in the 1570s, ordered a printing press from Copenhagen so that he could publish Lutheran texts such as his 1594 *Gradual* (4) for the local population.

While a few important works such as the Danish provincial laws were first written and published in the vernacular (5), most literary and scientific texts of the Renaissance were published in Latin, the international language of learning and scientific discourse. The poetry of Erasmus Laet and the great scientific treatises of Tycho Brahe, for example, are written in Latin. Nevertheless, the work of Christian Pedersen and other sixteenth-century humanists assured that the Danish language would emerge in the seventeenth century as the literary language of Denmark.

1
Saxo Grammaticus (ca. 1150–ca. 1220)   *Danorum Regu[m] Herou[m]q[ue] Historię*

Paris:
Iodocus Badius Ascensius,
1514

Referred to variously as *Gesta Danorum* and *Historia Danica*, this chronicle of Danish kings draws from many different legendary and popular sources. The first nine books create a lively and unified story of early Danish history from Dan to Gorm III. Among the many legends preserved is that of Hamlet the Danish prince. In the second part, Saxo brings the story of Denmark up to 1185, the date when he probably began writing his chronicle. Saxo was a cleric in the diocese of Lund in Skåne, an important center of medieval learning ceded to Sweden in 1658. In recognition of his ability as a Latinist, Saxo was called "Grammaticus," a name which now obscures his original family name "Lange."

More than three centuries later Christian Pedersen, a Danish scholar living in Paris, edited and published *Gesta Danorum* from a manuscript copy. The publication of this work, in a beautiful edition with specially commissioned ornamental initials, heralds the beginning of Danish Humanism.

1966—Purchased with the George L. Lincoln (HC 1895) Fund.

2
The Christian III Bible   *Biblia . . . den Gantske Hellige Scrifft . . . paa Danske*

Copenhagen: Ludowich Dietz,
1550

With the support of Christian III (1533–1559), Christian Pedersen edited and translated most of this first Bible in the Danish language. His translations of the Psalms are among his finest efforts. Having worked for several years in Paris and Holland to promote the cause of Danish literature and the Reformation, Pedersen returned to Denmark in 1531 where he remained until his death in 1554. Pedersen's 1550 Bible in idiomatic Danish is one of his two most important contributions to the development of the national literature.

Although the pictorial title borders and most of woodcuts had been used by Dietz in the Low German Bible (Lübeck 1533), the portrait of Christian III and the royal arms framed in ornamental detail were specially commissioned for this edition.

1984—Gift of Philip Hofer (HC 1921).

3
The Frederik II Bible   *Biblia . . . den Gantske Hellige Scrifft, paa Danske igen Offuerseet*

Copenhagen: Matz Vingaardt,
1589

This second edition of the Danish Bible by Mads Vingaard, one of the most important 16th-century printers, is here opened to the 23rd Psalm. Included in this edition is an engraving of Frederik II by Hendrik Goltzius, based on a painting by Ghert Cornelis.

1984—Gift of Philip Hofer (HC 1921).

4
Gudbrand Thorlaksson (1542–1627)   *Gradvale: ein Almen[n]eleg Messusöngs Bok*

Hólar in Hjalltadal:
Jon Jonsson,
1594

This Lutheran *Gradual* is a rare first edition, one of only about fifty texts published in Iceland before 1600. It includes examples of both earlier medieval and more modern forms of musical notation. On the verso of the title page is a woodcut of the Icelandic coat-of-arms, a gutted and crowned fish on a scroll shield.

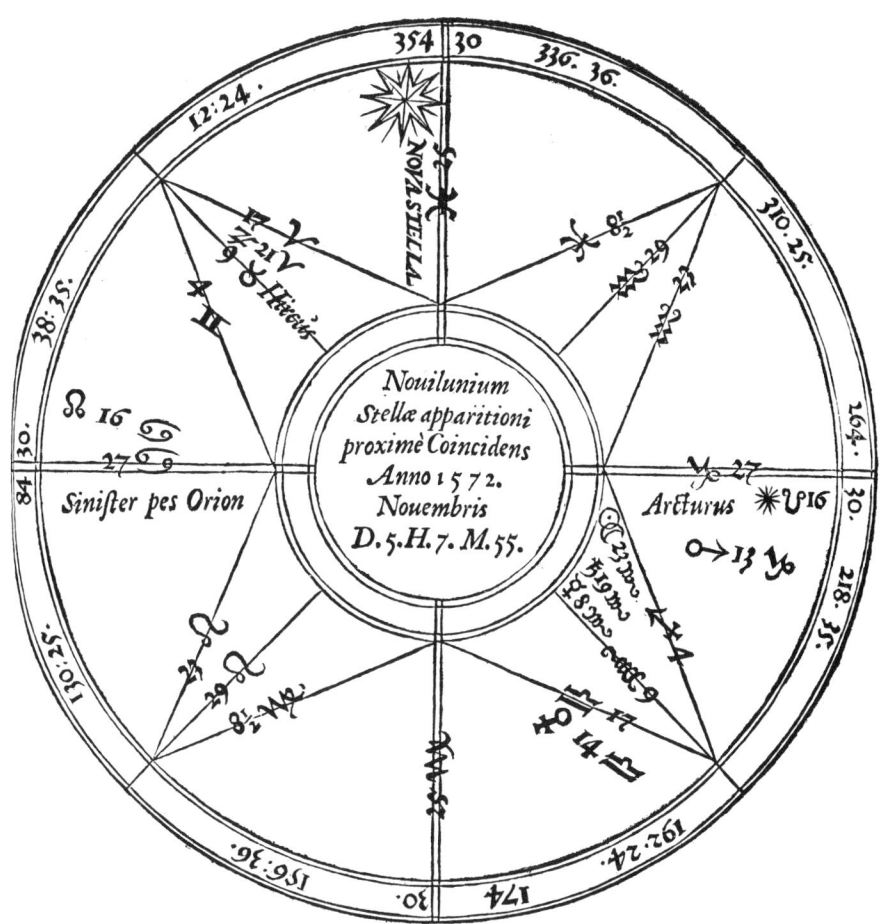

*vel non longè ante aut poſt , ſtellam primùm apparuiſſe
exiſtimo. Nobis enim , vt ab initio teſtatus ſum, primùm die 11 Nouembris conſpecta eſt: an verò aliquot
prius diebus fulſerit , quoniam in noſtra Regione dies*
             E   **illj**

6   Brahe   *De Nova Stella*   Copenhagen, 1573

Thorlaksson's *Gradual*, which is based on the Niels Jespersen Danish *Gradual* of 1573, went through nineteen editions until it was replaced by the 1801 hymnbook. In some churches in nineteenth-century Iceland, however, the Thorlaksson continued to be the preferred version. The worn and yellowed pages of this copy testify to its heavy use.

1904—Gift of Archibald Cary Coolidge (HC 1887).

5

Zealand Law of Valdemar the Great (r. 1157–1182)   *Haer Begynnes then Zelands Low paa Raet Dansk och Aer Skifft i Sÿw Bøgher . . .*

Copenhagen: Matz Wingaardt, 1576

Three provincial codes were developed in the late 12th and early 13th centuries, during the reign of the Valdemars: the Laws of Skåne, Zealand, and Jutland. These codes protected the rights of citizens and remained essentially unchallenged until the latter half of the 17th century when Frederik III asserted the absolute authority of the king's law, the "kongelov" (see *Lex regia* 24), and when Christian V published his *Danske lov*. While the Jutland Law is the most famous, all three are rich sources of information about provincial life and the local dialects of the Middle Ages.

The colophon indicates that this is the second edition of the Zealand Law, first published in 1505, to which are appended the "promissiones" of Kings Erik and Olof and the ecclesiastical law of Absalon, Archbishop of Lund and patron of Saxo Grammaticus. The 1505 woodblock-illustration on the first leaf of this copy has been handcolored.

In 1835 the young Henry Wadsworth Longfellow, who had just been offered a professorship of modern languages at Harvard, was traveling and studying in Germany and Scandinavia. This copy, which he found during his travels in Copenhagen, marks the beginning of Harvard's Scandinavian collection. The 1835 Longfellow bookplate is reproduced on the inside of the front cover of this exhibition catalogue.

1835—Gift of Henry Wadsworth Longfellow.

6

Tycho Brahe (1546–1601)   *De Nova . . . Stella . . . Contemplatio Mathematica*

Copenhagen: Laurentius Benedictus, 1573

When he was only fourteen years old, Tycho Brahe observed a total eclipse of the sun on 21 August 1560, the exact day on which astronomers had calculated it would occur. Inspired by this vivid illustration of the possibility of applied mathematics in astronomy, Brahe began to devote much of his time to the study of mathematics and the stars. Two years later he made his own first recorded observation, the conjunction of the planets Jupiter and Saturn. When he learned that existing chartings of the planets and stars were inaccurate, he decided to become an astronomer instead of a lawyer so that he could develop his own more accurate calculations. On 11 November 1572 he discovered a new star in the constellation of Cassiopeia—an exciting but unsettling discovery for an age which believed in the unchanging harmony of the spheres, a universe in which no new stars, by definition, could be discovered. Several months after this discovery, Brahe published his findings in this his most important and revolutionary work. Displaying his talent as a neo-Latin poet, Brahe ends *De nova stella* with a Latin poem dedicated to Urania, the Muse of Astronomy.

1986—Gift of Harrison Horblit (HC 1933).

7
Tycho Brahe (1546–1601) *Epistolarum Astronomicarum Libri*

Uraniborg [Ven]:
Author's private press,
1596

Tycho Brahe's *De nova stella* made him famous throughout most of Europe. In 1576 Frederik II gave him the island of Ven (or Hven, as it was then called) in the Sound, about halfway between Zealand and the coast of Skåne. Here Brahe built two great observatories, Uraniborg and Stjerneborg. At the former, named after Urania, he established a printing house where he published several of his own texts including these *Epistolae*. In the colophon to this work, Brahe has included his device, a woodcut of the classical figure of "Astronomy." This text is one of the last published at Ven before he went into exile in Germany for the remaining few years of his life.

In addition to an important Tycho Brahe collection, Houghton owns the original editions of two of his famous pupils — Christian Longberg (Longomontanus) and Johannes Kepler. It was Kepler who used many of Brahe's observations to develop his own theories which in turn revolutionized the study of astronomy.

This copy of Brahe's *Epistolae* belonged to the great German mathematician, Karl Gustav Jacob Jacobi (1804–1851).

1851 — Gift of Horace Appleton Haven (HC 1842).

8
Erasmus Michael Laet (1526–1582) *Margareticorum . . . Libri Decem*

Frankfort-on-the-Main:
Georgius Corvinus;
Sigismundus Feyerabend,
1573

Born "Rasmus Glad," Erasmus Laet published his poetical works under his Latin name. He was well-educated, widely traveled, and unusually prolific as a neo-Latin poet. Although rarely read today, Laet was in his time influential and held high favor in the royal court. His subject matter was often historical, designed particularly to flatter royalty.

This historical poem celebrates the achievements of Queen Margaret, the daughter of the third Valdemar and the great-granddaughter of Valdemar the Victorious. At the end of the fourteenth century, Margaret succeeded in driving the Germans from Sweden and was in turn recognized as Queen of Sweden. With her ties by marriage to Norway, Margaret created a powerful but delicately balanced union of Denmark, Norway, and Sweden which survived in name from 1397 to 1523.

In 1570, at the end of the Nordic Seven Years War, just before Laet published his *Margaretica*, Denmark had lost significant ground to the rising power of Sweden. Meanwhile, the power of Elizabeth of England was also on the rise. By dedicating to Elizabeth this celebration of a powerful Danish queen, Laet intended to flatter the English queen, perhaps to suggest a parallel between Margaret's Scandinavian union and Elizabeth's own efforts to unify her kingdom. The *Margaretica* is opened to this dedication and to Laet's own coat-of-arms, on the verso of the title page.

1978 — Purchased with the Amy Lowell Fund.

9
Erasmus Michael Laet (1526–1582) *Rerum Danicarum Libri Undecim*

Frankfort-on-the-Main:
Georgius Corvinus;
Sigismundus Feyerabend,
1574

Although largely imitative of Virgil and other classics, Laet's neo-Latin poetry retains in the descriptive passages some of the vivid local color of his native Jutland. This monumental work of more than 16,000 verses about "Danish matters" is probably his finest effort.

1965 — Purchased with the Amy Lowell Fund.

10   Syv   *Nogle Betenkninger om det Cimbriske Sprog*   Copenhagen, 1663

The Seventeenth Century

While many continued in the seventeenth century to write in Latin, a number of Danish poets and scholars showed a growing interest in their native tongue. Unlike Erasmus Laet, Peder Syv, the linguist, preferred the Danish to the Latin form of his name Septimus. Expanding the 1591 collection of Danish ballads, Syv continued the work of Pedersen and Vedel, providing renewed scholarly support for the literature of the vernacular. Anders Arrebo wrote his *Hexaëmeron* (14) in Danish verse, with an occasional lightness that suggests the rhythms of folk ballads. Anders Bording established the first Danish newspaper, and Thomas Kingo created some of the greatest and most enduring poetry in Danish literature. Leonora Christine Ulfeldt, the daughter of Christian IV, also showed some talent as a poet. She is now known, however, for her powerful "memoirs of suffering," written during her imprisonment from 1663 to 1685.

While Peder Syv helped to legitimize the contemporary use of the vernacular in literature, Ole Worm and his followers studied the origins of the Danish language, exploring Denmark's relationship to ancient runic inscriptions and the development of Icelandic literature. Archeologists and historians collected Danish and other Scandinavian artifacts, displaying them in private museums and theorizing about their significance for Denmark. Combing old manuscripts for stories of Danish kings, historians and poets composed new chronicles in the tradition of Saxo. The list of new Danish historians is long and includes names like Huitfeldt, Claussøn, Resen, Debes, Lyschander. Even Ludvig Holberg in the first part of the eighteenth century tried his hand at writing Danish history.

In this age of exploration and colonization, people were very interested in mapping and describing the distant regions of the Danish kingdom. The wild coasts of Greenland, the colorful Orkneys and Faroes, and, of course, Iceland were of great interest to historians, scientists and poets. In his magnificent eight-volume atlas of Denmark (33–36), the younger Erik Pontoppidan continues this tradition into the eighteenth century with his detailed descriptions and illustrations of the varying landscapes of Denmark.

10

Peder Pedersen Syv (1631–1702) *Nogle Betenkninger om det Cimbriske Sprog*

Copenhagen,
1663

Peder Syv is sometimes referred to as "the first Danish grammarian." In this remarkable little book, with its curious illustrated title page, Syv defends the use of the Danish language in literature. To demonstrate the strength of his native Danish tongue, Syv cites the accomplishments of important authors writing in Danish. A number of those he mentions are represented in this exhibition—for example, Huitfeldt, Skonning, Arrebo, Bording, and Pontoppidan.

1966—Purchased with the Fred N. Robinson Fund.

11

Peder Pedersen Syv (1631–1702) *Den Danske Sprog-Kunst eller Grammatica*

Copenhagen:
Johann Philip Bockenhoffer,
1685

This work by Syv is the first grammar in Danish. An earlier Danish grammar by the older of the two Erik Pontoppidans (12) is written in Latin. Ironically, while defending other writers' use of Danish in literature, Syv still finds it necessary to apologize for using Danish instead of Latin in his own grammar. Occasionally he provides a Latin translation, to make certain the reader can understand his analysis.

1884—Purchased with the Charles Minot (HC 1828) Fund.

12
Erik Pontoppidan (1616–1678)   *Grammatica Danica*

Copenhagen:
Christianus Veringius,
1668

Erik Pontoppidan's Danish grammar was published about twenty years earlier than Syv's. To explain the linguistic structure of Danish, Pontoppidan felt he had to rely on Latin, which was still the international language of learning — the language which Ole Worm and others used in explaining runic inscriptions and in analyzing Icelandic texts (18). The main interest of Pontoppidan's grammar is that it uses comparative philology to analyze the Danish language.

1969 — Purchased with the Keller Fund.

13
Anders Sørensen Vedel (1542–1616); Peder Pedersen Syv (1631–1702), editors
Et Hundrede Udvalde Danske Viser

Copenhagen:
Johann Philip Bockenhoffer,
1695

In addition to writing the two linguistic studies described above (10, 11), Peder Syv published this important edition of early Danish ballads and folksongs. In 1591, sixteen years after publishing the first Danish translation of Saxo, Anders Sørensen Vedel edited the first major collection of old and contemporary ballads. In this edition a hundred years later, Syv expands the Vedel collection, adding his own findings. Houghton also holds Syv's first expanded edition of Vedel's original and unique collection of Danish proverbs.

More than one hundred and fifty years after Syv's edition, Svend Grundtvig, the son of N. F. S. Grundtvig, began a second major revised and expanded edition of Vedel's original collection, an edition which remains even today the standard source of Danish ballads and folksongs.

1884 — Purchased with the Charles Minot (HC 1828) Fund.

14
Anders Christensen Arrebo (1587–1637)   *Hexaëmeron Rhythmico-Danicum*

Copenhagen: Hendrick Gøde,
1661

In 1623 Anders Arrebo published a free translation of the Psalms which proved to be very popular. His most important literary contribution, however, is his version of the *Hexaëmeron*, which he composed in Danish instead of the traditional Latin. Written in loose imitation of the earlier (1578) French version (*La sepmaine* by Du Bartas), Arrebo describes in free epic verse the six days of the Creation. The first part of his poem is in hexameter, with caesurae and rhyming patterns at the middle and end of each line. For the remaining parts, however, Arrebo abandons this inflexible meter and uses a freer alexandrine form modeled after the German rather than the French epic line.

While serving as Bishop of Trondheim, Arrebo acquired a special taste for folksongs and popular dances. Because of his interest in such non-clerical forms, Arrebo was dismissed from his post. Despite his use of intricate artifice, Arrebo's poetry reveals the refreshing influence of the lively rhythms of Danish popular song and dance.

1901 — Gift of Mrs. E. C. Hammer, in memory of Emil Christian Hammer.

15
Hans Hansen Skonning (1579–1651)   *Kattenis Raettergang med Hundene*

Aarhus: Author's Press,
1650

A contemporary of Arrebo, Skonning is today an obscure figure. In his lifetime, however, he was well-known as a poet and a printer. This first edition of his *Kattenis raettergang med Hundene*, an allegorical verse epic with prose commentary, is a relatively rare seventeenth-century Aarhus imprint, published at the author's own printing house. Each page of text is printed within a border of type ornaments.

1969 — Gift of Christian A. Zabriskie, in memory of Edward Powis Jones (HC 1940).

12 Pontoppidan *Grammatica Danica* Copenhagen, 1668   17 Bartholin *De Scriptis Danorum* Copenhagen, 1666

16
Anders Bording (1619–1677) *Poëtiske Skrifter*

Copenhagen:
Kongl. Privilegerede
Bogtrykkerie,
1735

Two poets, Thomas Kingo and Anders Bording, are noteworthy representatives of the seventeenth-century baroque. Kingo, Bishop of Odense, is the more enduring of the two. Several of his impassioned hymns are popular even today. But during his lifetime, Bording was a favorite. Although his style is inflated with the exaggerations of the high-baroque, Bording manages to capture in many of his poems some of the charm and playfulness of the Danish folk song. As is typical of poets of this era, Bording wrote both religious and secular verse. While Kingo is known for his hymns, Bording is more successful as an occasional poet and satirist. Perhaps his most important contribution to Danish literature is his creation of what is called "the first Danish newspaper," *Den danske Mercurius* (1666–1677). This monthly gazette is written in alexandrines and comments ironically on the political events of the day.

The 1735 edition, which includes *Den danske Mercurius*, is the first complete collection of Bording's poetry; it also represents the first collected edition of any Danish poet.

1835—Purchased by Henry Wadsworth Longfellow.

17
Albert Bartholin (1620–1663), Thomas Bartholin (1616–1680) editor
De Scriptis Danorum

Copenhagen:
Matthias Godicchenius;
Petrus Haubold,
1666

With Tycho Brahe, Hans Christian Ørsted, and Niels Bohr, Denmark has produced more than its share of internationally famous scientists. Others, while not as famous, have also made important contributions. Among these are the seventeenth-century scientists Simon Paulli, Niels Steensen, Ole Rømer, and the Bartholin family. The Bartholins, known primarily for their contributions to anatomy, include Kaspar senior, his sons Thomas and Albert, and Thomas' own son, Kaspar. The most famous of these is Thomas, who is known as the one who discovered the lymphatic system. Thomas was also a literary scholar. When his younger brother Albert died at forty-three before finishing his bibliography of Danish writers, Thomas took over the project and had it published in 1666. This book is a remarkable record of Danish literature from its early days to the middle of the seventeenth century. The Bartholins list over 500 authors and more than 1000 different titles.

This bibliography is not the first such effort. A number of years before the Bartholins, Claus Christoffersen Lyschander compiled his own list of mostly sixteenth-century Danish authors, *De scriptoribus Danicis libellus*. The Lyschander list was not published until 1739, and so it is the Bartholin bibliography which is usually cited. In two early eighteenth-century bibliographies—a list of Dano-Norwegian historians and a list of Danish women writers (26)—Bartholin is given as the bibliographical authority.

1963—Purchased with the Susan A. E. Morse Fund.

18
Ole Worm (1588–1654) *Danica Literatura Antiquissima*

Copenhagen:
Melchiorus Martzan,
1636

While Peder Syv defends the use of Danish in contemporary literature, Ole Worm and his followers explore the roots of the Danish language, its literature and cultural monuments. Like the Bartholins, Ole Worm was trained formally as a physician and published studies in medicine. But his true love was archeology, and it is in this field that Worm made his most important contributions.

Worm collected and studied runic inscriptions and manuscripts in Old Icelandic and Old Danish. He was the first to publish Old Icelandic texts, which he found in manuscript form. In this 1636 first edition of his important study of runic literature, Worm provides the Old Icelandic text in runic letters, with parallel Latin translations, of *Krákumál* (originally thought to be by Ragnar Lodbrók) and *Höfudlausn*, by Egill Skallagrímsson. He also adds, without a translation, an Old Icelandic list of skalds, the *Skáldatal*.

Although the Old Icelandic literary manuscripts he published did not contain runic letters, Worm assumed — as did other runologists at the time — that Icelandic literature must have been written originally in runes. Therefore, after studying the various forms of the runic alphabet, Worm felt quite free to transcribe the texts into runic letters in his efforts to reconstruct what he thought to be their original form. It is now recognized, however, that Worm was mistaken in this assumption. No runic manuscripts which date before 1300 have yet been found in Iceland. Runes were apparently used throughout Scandinavia for magic or rituals, not for recording the literature of the oral tradition.

1984 — Purchased with the Amy Lowell Fund.

19
Magnús Ólafsson (1573 – 1636) *Specimen Lexici Runici*

Copenhagen:
Melchiorus Martzan,
1650

Ole Worm was the first scholar to publish a runic dictionary or glossary of selected runic terms. This glossary, provided by the Icelandic scholar Magnús Ólafsson, is intended as an aid to the study of Old Icelandic literature.

The renaissance in Old Icelandic studies at the end of the seventeenth and the beginning of the eighteenth centuries is largely the result of the initial inspiration provided by Ole Worm. Worm's correspondence with Icelandic scholars such as Ólafsson is voluminous. It is evident that his energy and enthusiasm inspired Icelanders and Danes alike to study early Scandinavian literature. His own collection of manuscripts was passed on to Arni Magnússon, who became the greatest collector of Icelandic manuscripts. While Magnússon lost many items in the 1728 Copenhagen fire, a number survived and can be studied today in the Arni Magnússon Institute.

18th century — Gift of Thomas Hollis.

20
Ole Worm (1588 – 1654) *Fasti Danici*

Copenhagen:
Joachimus Moltkenius,
1643

Ole Worm's earliest archeological study is his *Fasti Danici*, originally published in 1626. Houghton holds the second and third editions, 1633 and 1643, of this work. In this study Worm describes, with numerous illustrations, various Old Danish calendars discovered by runologists. The 1643 edition shown here was bound in the early eighteenth century for the famous French book collector, Henri-Louis de Loménie Comte de Brienne, whose coat-of-arms is stamped in gold on the covers.

1984 — Gift of Philip Hofer (HC 1921).

21
Ole Worm (1588 – 1654) *Danicorum Monumentorum Libri Sex* in *Antiquitates Danicae*

Copenhagen:
Joachimus Moltkenius,
1643

The *Monumenta* is Worm's largest and probably his greatest work. It is a comprehensive study with numerous illustrations of the Danish runic inscriptions known to Worm and other runologists of the time. Worm worked for many years on this study, collecting materials and making sketches. Originally the illustrations were to be engraved; but, to minimize printing costs, woodcuts were used instead. Many of the cuts were made by Worm himself; others were by the students and collectors assisting him.

Near the end of the *Monumenta Danica*, Worm includes a revised version of his *Cornu aureum Danicum*, originally published in 1641. (The Houghton copy of the first edition is bound with *Specimen runici* 19.) The *Cornu* includes a four-panel engraving, after a drawing by Worm, of the golden horn discovered in 1639 in southern Jutland not far from Tønder. As part of some kind of ritual, the horn had been buried during the period of the Great Migration of the Nordic tribes, probably in the fifth century A.D. Its discovery excited the minds and hearts of poets and scholars. Worm was one of the first to provide a meticulous description of the horn, ring by ring, detail by detail.

1904—Gift of Archibald Cary Coolidge (HC 1887).

22
Ole Worm (1588–1654)   *Museum Wormianum, seu Historia Rerum Rariorum*

Leyden: Johannes Elsevirius, 1665

This work includes a detailed description of the items Ole Worm collected and preserved in his private museum. The artifacts and specimens described in *Museum* demonstrate that Worm not only was an archeologist but also a natural scientist interested in comparative anatomy. The two-page engraving by the Dutch artist G. Wingendorp of Worm's museum shows the exhibition room crowded with a wide variety of specimens.

The printer for this edition is Johannes Elsevir of Leyden. Houghton also has another issue of this edition by Daniel Elsevir of Amsterdam.

Old purchase.

23
Ole Worm (1588–1654)   *Regum Daniae Series Duplex et Limitum inter Daniam &*
Sveciam Descriptio

Copenhagen: Melchiorus Martzan; Joachimus Moltkenius, 1642

Ole Worm gives these two lists of Danish kings in both Latin and Old Danish, in runic letters. The *Series duplex* is one of several works found in the "Codex Runicus," a manuscript from about 1300. As indicated by Worm on the title page, the Codex also contains the old Scanian Law, the Scanian Ecclesiastical Law, and a document describing the boundaries between Denmark and Sweden. At the end of his *Series duplex* Worm includes the description of the Dano-Swedish boundaries.

This copy is bound with several other works by Worm, in full eighteenth-century sheep. On the front fly-leaf, N. F. S. Grundtvig has signed his name with an inscription and the date 1816. At the bottom of the same leaf, his son Svend Grundtvig, scholar and collector of Danish ballads, added his own autograph in 1872. It is appropriate that these three important figures in Danish cultural history, Ole Worm, N. F. S. and Svend Grundtvig, are linked through this volume. The senior Grundtvig—politician, historian, educator, theologian, and poet—has been at least as influential as Ole Worm in many areas of Danish life. In 1816 Grundtvig was working on his translations of Snorri and Saxo (63). In 1872 N. F. S. Grundtvig died and Svend, who had just completed more than three volumes of his collection of Danish ballads, added his father's books to his own library.

The younger Grundtvig has a Harvard connection. Professor F. J. Child, who produced the standard collection of English and Scottish ballads, based his scholarship on Grundtvig. During the early 1880s, Child and Grundtvig exchanged information about ballads.

1884—Purchased with the Charles Minot (HC 1828) Fund.

20 Worm *Fasti Danici* Copenhagen, 1643

21   Worm   *Danicorum Monumentorum Libri Sex*   Copenhagen, 1643

24
Kongelov of Frederik III (r. 1648–1670)   *Lex Regia*

[Copenhagen, 1709]

For nearly five centuries, from the time of Valdemar I when the first provincial laws were promulgated, the rights of individual citizens were upheld by succeeding monarchies. The laws stated that even the will of the king was not to obstruct these basic rights. In the 1660s, however, during a time of turmoil when Denmark was being outmaneuvered politically and militarily by Sweden, a new royal law was instituted. This law established the absolute right of the monarch to rule and defined the line of royal succession. This affirmation of absolute authority was more rigorous than other monarchal laws of Europe at the time.

The *Lex regia* or *Kongelov* was drafted originally in 1660 by Count Peder Griffenfeld and then formalized by Frederik III in 1665, two years after he had thrown his own sister, Leonora Christine, into prison without trial. Except for an extract included in Christian V's 1683 law, the *Lex regia* was not formally printed until 1709 during the reign of Frederik IV, well after the death of Frederik III. The publication was limited to 500 copies, reserved mostly for monarchs and nobles.

The title and text of this handsome volume are engraved throughout by Michael Røg. The elaborate illustrated borders, which appear on every page, are engraved by Anders Reinhardt after designs by Claus à Möinichen. The illustrations depict the various colonial and industrial interests of Denmark at this time. In addition to the 1709 title page, there is a special title page for the date of 1665 when the law was first instituted. Following this special title is an engraved portrait head of Frederik III with a calligraphic body, seated on a calligraphic horse.

Inserted opposite each leaf in this copy is a manuscript English translation by Jenkin Thomas Philipps, in ornamental script and dated 1720. This copy is bound, with gilt edges, in contemporary calf.

1915—Gift of Daniel B. Fearing (HC 1882).

25
Leonora Christine Ulfeldt (1621–1698)   *Jammersminde*

Copenhagen: Gyldendal, 1869

When she was only fifteen Leonora Christine, daughter of Christian IV, married the Count Corfitz Ulfeldt. The count was given extensive powers during the reign of Christian IV, but was stripped of these powers by the next king, Leonora's half brother Frederik III. In rebellion Corfitz traveled to Sweden, Holland, and Germany, where he engaged in a series of unsuccessful intrigues against Frederik. Corfitz's young wife, ever faithful to her husband, followed him wherever he went. In 1663 she went to England to collect money owed to Corfitz. Instead of returning the money, Charles II handed her over to the Danes, to gain political favor with Frederik. In Copenhagen she was thrown into prison, and her husband, who had escaped to a distant island, was sentenced to death *in absentia*.

Leonora Christine remained in prison for twenty-two years without trial. Had it been his decision alone, Frederik III might not have allowed her to languish for so many years. But his queen, Sophie Amalie, was bitterly envious of the talented Leonora Christine, and it was mostly to appease her that Leonora was so callously treated.

Leonora Christine was known in her time as a poet. The 1732 bibliography of Danish women writers includes her name and quotes several lines from her poetry (26). It is as a prose writer, however, that she is now celebrated. Towards the end of her imprisonment, Leonora Christine wrote a memoir of her years of suffering, *Jammersminde*. When she died thirteen years after being released, the manuscript was preserved by her descendants, the Austrian noble family of Waldstein. *Jammersminde* was unknown to the general public until 1869 when it was edited

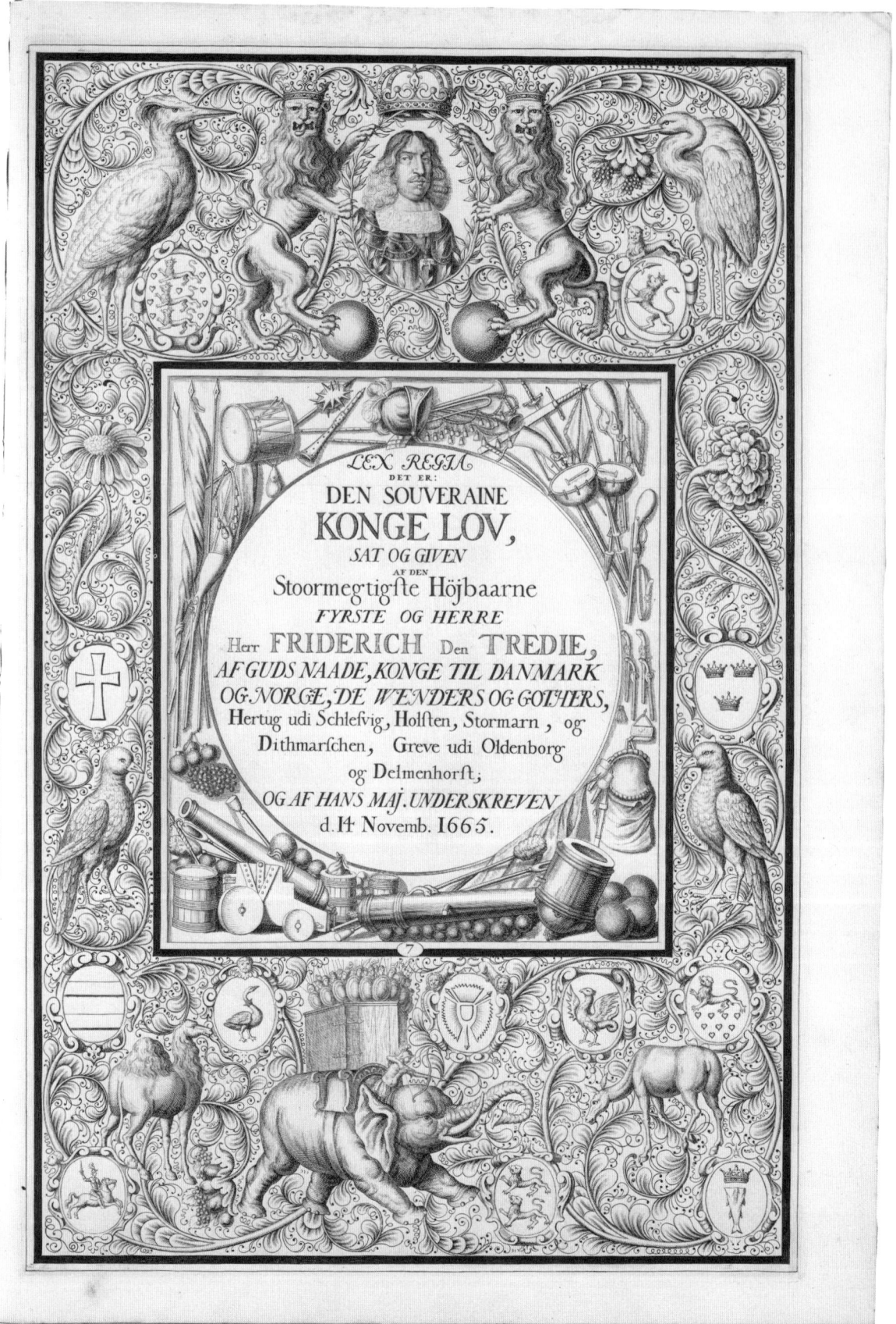

24   Frederik III *Lex Regia* Copenhagen, 1709

and published by Sophus Birkett Smith. The use of vivid detail, the depth of feeling and skill in composition have made these memoirs popular and enduring as great literature. Leonora Christine Ulfeldt now stands out as one of the very best writers of the seventeenth century.

The first printing of only a few copies in June of 1869 sold out almost immediately, and a second printing was released in October 1869. Houghton's copy is from this second run.

1962 — Purchased with the Archibald Cary Coolidge (HC 1887) and Clarence Leonard Hay (HC 1908) Fund.

26
Albert Thura (1700–1740) *Gynaeceum Daniae Litteratum*

Altona: Jonus Kortus,
1732

This interesting bibliography lists a surprisingly large number of Danish women writers known at the time of its publication. In addition to being treated to a few lines from Leonora Christine's poetry, we learn, for example, that Tycho Brahe's sister, Sophia, was an accomplished poet.

1978 — Purchased with the Amy Lowell Fund.

27
Arild Huitfeldt (1546–1609) *En Kaart Historiske Beskriffuelse . . . under Kong Christian den Tredje . . .*

Copenhagen: Matz Vingaard,
1595

After publishing his translation of Saxo Grammaticus, Vedel was asked to continue Saxo's work and to bring the study of Denmark down to his own time. There were disagreements about how thorough this history should be and which language should be used, Danish or Latin. The project was then given with Vedel's notes to another historian, who accomplished little, and finally to Arild Huitfeldt.

Huitfeldt worked quickly, from 1595 to 1603, providing nine volumes of Danish history from King Dan I down to 1559 and the reign of Christian III. He published the ninth volume first (1595) which is the volume on display in this exhibition. In 1604 he added a tenth volume, a chronicle of Danish bishops.

Huitfeldt had hoped to create a more carefully written version of his history, but he died before he had the chance. Although rough in some places, this work provides an invaluable source of information not otherwise available. For example, it contains the text of original documents, letters, and descriptions of laws. This volume includes a copy of the portrait of Christian III commissioned for the 1550 Bible.

1968 — Purchased with the George L. Lincoln (HC 1898) Fund.

28
Arild Huitfeldt (1546–1609) *Danmarckis Rigis Krønicke*

Copenhagen: Joachim
Moltken, 1652–[1655].

In this edition, the complete Huitfeldt Danish history and the chronicle of bishops are published in two volumes. The title page of the first volume is engraved with figures representing the span of monarchs from King Dan to Christian IV. This edition also includes a fine portrait of Huitfeldt by Albert Haelwegh and a special title page for each part.

1904 — Gift of Archibald Cary Coolidge (HC 1887).

29
Claus Christoffersen Lyschander (1558–1624)   *Synopsis Historiarum Danicarum*

Copenhagen:
Henrich Waldkirch,
1622

The seventeenth century saw a number of outstanding historians who tried their literary talents at composing chronicles. In addition to Huitfeldt, these poet-historians include Peder Claussøn, Stephan Stephanius, Peder Resen, and Claus Lyschander. Not content simply to pick up where Huitfeldt left off, Lyschander tries to show a direct line of Danish kings from Adam and Eve, Noah and the Flood, right down to Christian IV. He presents his royal genealogy as historical fact, intimating that he has based the dates for his Biblical generations on old documents. The *Synopsis* is intended as a sourcebook for historians and is of interest today for its carefully wrought and intricate style.

1904—Gift of Archibald Cary Coolidge (HC 1887).

30
Claus Christoffersen Lyschander (1558–1624)   *Den Grønlandske Chronica*

Copenhagen:
Benedicht Laurentz
1608

In this chronicle Lyschander has created an epic poem of nearly 7000 lines in six-line stanzas (aabccb). He describes the history of Greenland from its earliest settlements to the expeditions of Christian IV between 1605 and 1607. His vivid descriptive verse captures the excitement of travel to these remote regions of the Danish kingdom.

1904—Gift of Archibald Cary Coolidge (HC 1887).

31
Thormod Torfaeus (1636–1719)   *Orcades*

Copenhagen: Justinus Hög,
1697

Torfaeus, scholar and archeologist, was appointed royal antiquarian and sent on expeditions to Iceland to find old manuscripts. He also was named royal historian of Norway, and completed a four-volume history of that country. Using his Icelandic sources, Torfaeus created a list of ancient Danish kings which differs from that of Saxo Grammaticus. Torfaeus' work caused some controversy but brought him fame.

   Torfaeus also wrote important histories of Greenland, the Faroes, and the Orkneys. In this study of the Orkneys he shows the history of the relationship of these islands to Denmark from the earliest times to the end of the seventeenth century.

1904—Gift of Archibald Cary Coolidge (HC 1887).

32
Lucas Jacobsøn Debes (1623–1675)   *Faeroae & Faeroa Reserata*

Copenhagen:
Matthias Jørgensøn,
1673

While some seventeenth-century scholars analyzed the history of these distant regions of the Danish kingdom, others were more interested in describing the contemporary physical and cultural setting. The geographical study of the Faroe Islands by Lucas Jacobsøn Debes is a good example of this kind of descriptive writing. Although more a scientist than a poet, Debes' use of vivid detail in describing the Faroes sparks the imagination of the reader. He explores not only the more mundane details of climate and population, but also the secrets of ghosts and satanic spirits. Yet as the detailed language of the title page indicates, Debes tried to be as scientific as possible. Although fascinated by the superstitions of the islands, he was a good rationalist, determined "to bring the mysteries to light."

   This copy has a folding woodcut chart which depicts the wind and weather patterns of part of the Faroes.

1904—Gift of Archibald Cary Coolidge (HC 1887).

28 Huitfeldt *Danmarckis Rigis Krønicke* Copenhagen, 1652-5

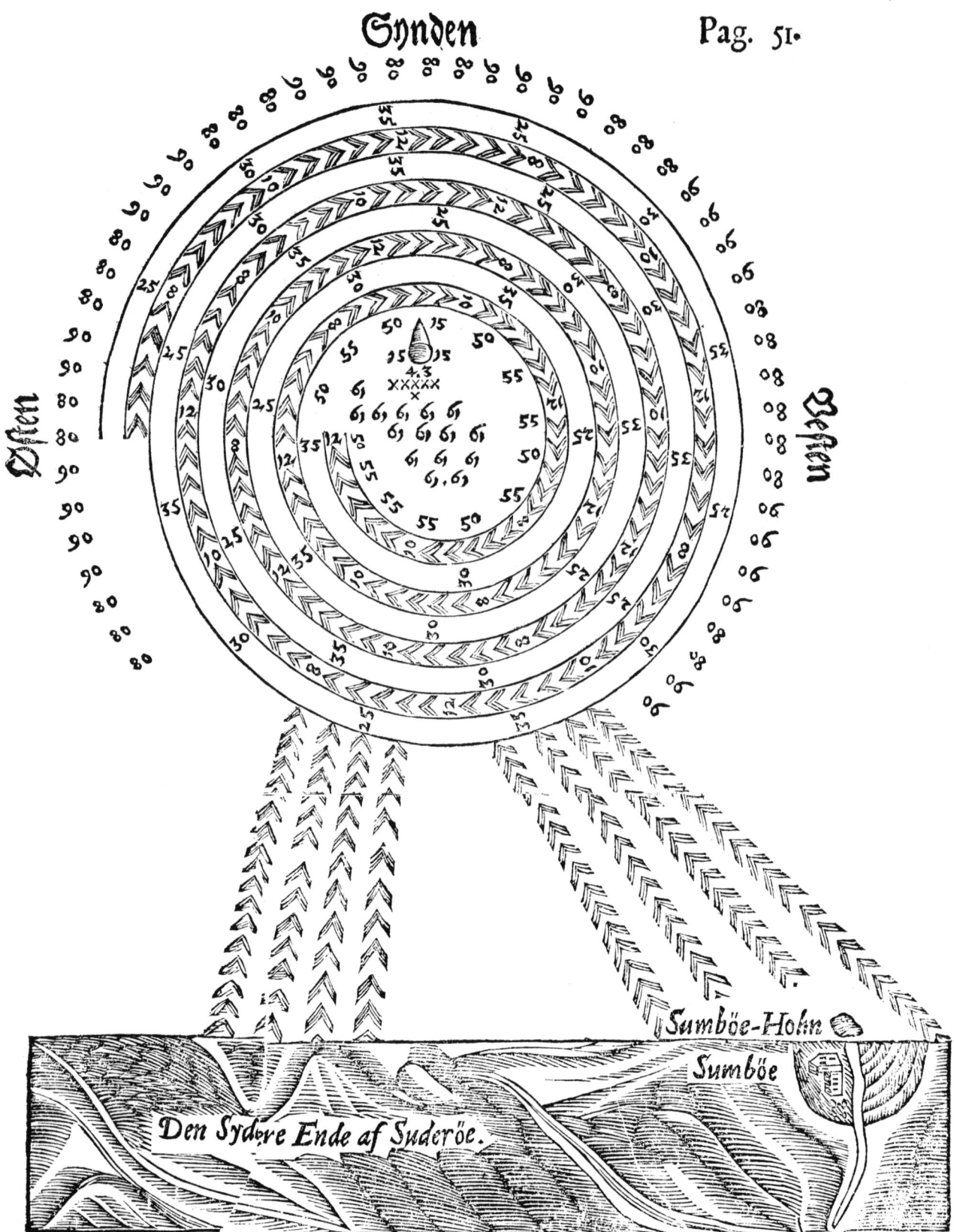

32   Debes   *Faeroae & Faeroa Reserata*   Copenhagen, 1673

Holberg and Classicism

For more than four centuries, from 1380 to 1814, Norway was a part of Denmark. The two countries were unified culturally as well as politically. Throughout this period a number of accomplished writers were born in Norway and later moved to Denmark. The most famous of these is Ludvig Holberg, born in Bergen in 1684. He was educated and lived most of his life in Copenhagen and is therefore considered both a Dane and a Norwegian.

Holberg was the first Danish author to achieve an international reputation and to be translated in many different languages. Great writers before Holberg—Saxo, Vedel, Kingo, Syv and others—made it possible for Holberg to develop his distinctive and "truly Danish" style. But it was not really until Holberg that Danes gained confidence in their language and began to think of Denmark as more than a satellite of the great literary schools of France, England, and Germany. Before Holberg, the educated Dane was expected to write his dissertations and essays in the international language of Latin. Any attempts at *belles lettres* were expected to defer to the French, English, or German models. Even Vedel, who loved the Danish language and who helped to preserve its folk literature, was afraid that if he wrote only in Danish he would be isolated from the European community of scholars.

Holberg studied and traveled in Oxford, Paris, and Rome and was greatly influenced by writers like Swift, Boileau, and Molière. Nevertheless, he was not one to imitate the writings of others. Proud and confident of his own vision, he created a whole new body of literature. A master of many forms, Holberg excelled in satirical fiction, the epistolary essay, and comic drama. His greatest works include *Peder Paars*, *Niels Klim*, the various moral essays, and the many comedies which are still performed today. Holberg gained international recognition during his lifetime and was given the honorary title of Baron in 1747 by Frederik V.

The spirit of Holberg remains classical. He had faith in the rational and moral directive of literature, and he preferred restrained and logical forms. Molière, not Shakespeare, was the inspiration for his comedies. Holberg was first and foremost a philosopher and educator. He believed that literature should instruct as well as entertain.

33
Erik Pontoppidan (1698–1764)

Copenhagen: A. H. Godiche, 1763

Den Danske Atlas Vol. I

One of the most useful sources for historians trying to reconstruct early eighteenth-century life in urban and provincial Denmark is Erik Pontoppidan's *Danish Atlas*. Houghton Library has all eight volumes, published between 1763 and 1781. The first three volumes were completed by Pontoppidan before his death, and the remaining five were edited by Hans de Hoffman.

In the first volume Pontoppidan gives a quick overview of the early history and setting of Denmark. As a footnote to the work of the great seventeenth-century archeologists, he provides his own description and illustration of such famous discoveries as the Jelling Stone. He also adds new information; for example, he describes the second golden horn found in 1734, eighty years after the death of Ole Worm.

This second horn, often referred to as "the shorter horn," is inscribed with a message in runes: "I Hlewagastir, son of Holt, have this horn made." From the style of the runes, scholars have been able to determine that the two golden horns were made during the fifth century A.D.

1965—Purchased with the Archibald Cary Coolidge (HC 1887) Fund.

34

Erik Pontoppidan (1698–1764)   *Den Danske Atlas* Vol. 5, Pt. 2

Copenhagen:
Andreas Hartvig Godiche,
1769

The other seven volumes of the *Atlas* contain wonderfully detailed descriptions of the villages, towns, and cities of the provinces of Denmark. Each town is given its own section, with at least one plate and a street map. In describing the town Pontoppidan uses a chatty style, drawing the reader into the setting. Like a good tourist guide, he describes the streets and shops, gives some of the local history, names famous people associated with the town, and reports on anything of human interest.

For example we learn that the town of Veile was chartered in 1503 and that its old name was Vedel. The name Vedel comes from the surname of the Vedel family, who helped to build the town. The most famous member of the family, Anders Vedel, grew up here before seeking his fortune in the big city. We also learn that many kings are associated with Veile, from Harald Bluetooth (the Viking king who had the Jelling Stone inscribed) to Christian VI.

1965 — Purchased with the Archibald Cary Coolidge (HC 1887) Fund.

35

Erik Pontoppidan (1698–1764)   *Den Danske Atlas* Vol. 2

Copenhagen:
Andreas Hartvig Godiche,
1764

The second volume of the *Atlas* is devoted to Copenhagen. It has over seventy illustrations and maps of different parts of the city. These city views provide a vivid picture of early eighteenth-century Copenhagen. Not only do they depict the buildings and streets, but they also show the way people of different classes dressed and carried on their daily activities. There are a number of lively scenes of the harbor, the parks, and city squares. Pontoppidan's view of the 1748 Royal Theatre is often reproduced in theatre history books.

One of the most important squares is Kongens Nytorv, a busy commercial and cultural center. It is here that the 1748 Royal Theatre was built, and it is here that fifty years later the great philosopher, Søren Kierkegaard, was born.

1965 — Purchased with the Archibald Cary Coolidge (HC 1887) Fund.

36

Erik Pontoppidan (1698–1764)   *Den Danske Atlas* Vol. 3

Copenhagen:
Andreas Hartvig Godiche,
1767

The third volume of Pontoppidan's *Atlas* is open to a view of the important town of Odense on the island of Fyn. Just fifty years after this illustration was published, the famous writer of tales and contemporary of Kierkegaard, Hans Christian Andersen, was a twelve-year old boy in Odense. The old medieval town had not changed much in fifty years from the time of Pontoppidan. In the notes to his tales, Andersen explains that many of his memories of Odense are incorporated in his stories. For example, his vivid memory of the generosity of his mother, who had "once upon a time" defended a poor drunken washerwoman of Odense, is recreated in his tale *Hun duede ikke* (*She Was No Good*).

1965 — Purchased with the Archibald Cary Coolidge (HC 1887) Fund.

37

Ludvig Holberg (1684–1754)   *Moralske Kierne*

Copenhagen:
Johan Kruse; Ove Lynnov,
1715

Holberg began his writing career in 1711 with a work of scholarship, *Introduction til de fornemste Europaeiske Rigers Historier* (*Introduction to the History of the Leading European Powers*). His second work, *Introduction til Naturens- og Folke-rettens Kundskab* (*Introduction to the Science of Natural Law and the Law of Nations*), was written while he was a student at the

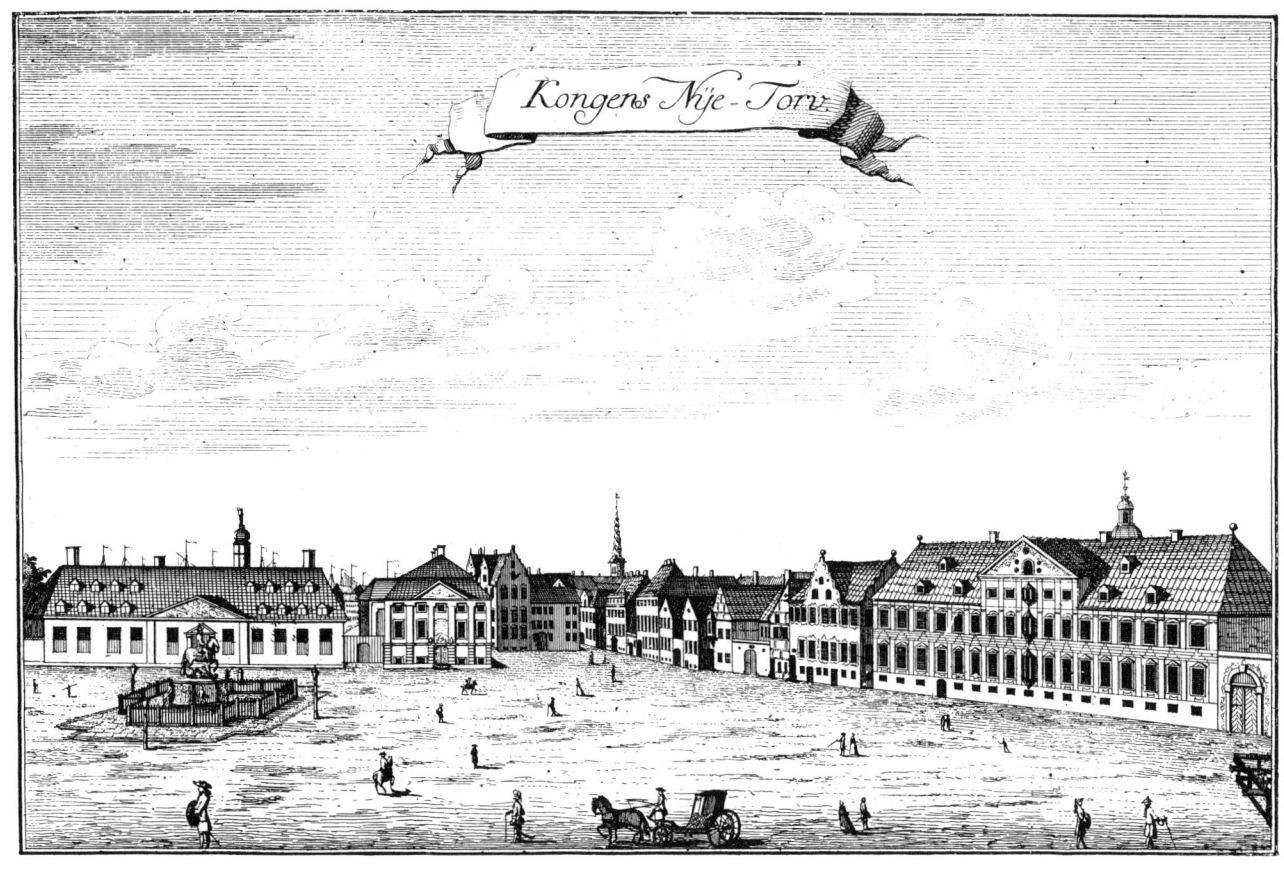

Kongens Nÿe-Torv.

35 Pontoppidan *Den Danske Atlas* Vol. 2 Copenhagen, 1764

University of Copenhagen. Later he added a second preface and changed the title to *Moralske Kierne*. This treatise on natural law and the rights of individuals was important in introducing the ideas of Hugo Grotius and Samuel Pufendorf to Scandinavia. It also contains Holberg's own thoughts on education in which he emphasizes that the moral development of the individual should be the most important goal of a school curriculum.

1968—Purchased with the George L. Lincoln (HC 1895) Fund.

38
Ludvig Holberg (1684–1754) *Ludvig Holbergs Trende Epistle . . . Hvorudi Befattes det Fornemske af Hans Liv og Levnet*

Copenhagen:
Ernst-Henrich Berling,
1745

In the style of the eighteenth-century periodical the *Spectator*, Holberg develops his own form of epistolary essay, the moral-philosophical essay. Many of the moral precepts he had argued so effectively in his youthful essay on natural law are put to specific and practical use in his five volumes of *Epistles* (1748–1754). These mature essays, full of the wisdom of years and covering a variety of topics, are spiced with the biting wit of an accomplished satirist. Holberg first used the epistolary form in his autobiographical memoirs—*Epistola ad virum perillustrem* (1728), *Epistola secunda* (1737), and *Epistola tertia* (1743). From these epistolary memoirs, with the addition of six philosophical essays, Holberg developed his great *Moralske Tanker* (*Moral Thoughts*, 1744).

This Danish version of the *Epistola tertia*, prepared with E. H. Berling, contains a frontispiece portrait of Holberg by J. B. Brühl.

1900—Gift of Mrs. E. C. Hammer, in memory of Emil Christian Hammer.

39
Ludvig Holberg (1684–1754) *Peder Paars*

Copenhagen:
Godiche; Et Selskab,
1772

In 1719 Holberg was thirty-five and had not yet written any of the plays or satirical works which would make him famous. He began writing satires in response to the harsh criticism of his works on natural law. His particular target was the scholar Andreas Højer. Inspired by the success of his satirical essays, Holberg began writing *Peder Paars*, an epic poem satirizing academia and other scholarly institutions. The first four episodes appeared in 1719 under his pseudonym Hans Mikkelsen, and the remaining three appeared soon after. *Peder Paars* satirizes the pedantry and pettiness of scholars who get caught up in silly, selfish pursuits.

In 1722 *Paars* was published for the first time in one volume. The original illustrations for the first edition are rather crude woodcuts. New illustrations were created for this later edition by Johan Frederik Clemens, after Johannes Wiedewelt and Peder Als. On the title page, the imprint information indicates that this 1772 edition was printed by the Godiche Press under the sponsorship of "Et Selskab." Among the several members of this society are the artist Johannes Wiederwelt and the poet and famous book collector, Bolle Willum Luxdorph.

1966—Gift of the Friends of the Harvard College Library.

40
Bolle Willum Luxdorph (1716–1788) *Carmina*

Copenhagen:
A. H. Godiche; F. C. Godiche,
1775

The height of classical design in Denmark is represented in this exhibition by the 1775 first edition of Bolle Willum Luxdorph's *Carmina*. A bibliophile and member of the Society which sponsored the fine illustrated 1772 edition of *Peder Paars* (39), B. W. Luxdorph was also a skilful poet. As the Latin title of this collection of poetry suggests, he was interested in and experimented with a variety of classical forms. The printing itself

39   Holberg   *Peder Paars*   Copenhagen, 1772

40 Luxdorph *Carmina* Copenhagen, 1775

is in the classical style, with an engraved title-vignette and two engraved illustrations by Jonas Haas and J. M. Preissler.

The binding of this copy is also a piece of fine workmanship. It was crafted by J. T. Wilhelms especially for Luxdorph and has Luxdorph's elephant-head device stamped in gold on the front cover. The image of the elephant is not uncommon in Danish illustration, especially in heraldic devices and other insignia. In the illustrated borders of *Lex regia* (24), for example, the elephant motif appears almost as frequently as the fish imagery. The elephant, seemingly an unlikely symbol for a Nordic country, alludes to the mythical story of the origin of the Danish flag, the "Dannebrog." In 1219, as the story goes, Danish forces were near defeat in Estonia—a battle in which elephants were reportedly used. Praying for guidance, the Danes were saved by the intervention of the Norse gods, who symbolically presented them from the skies with the red-and-white Danish flag. The image of the elephant therefore suggests this heroic past and the special grace of a chosen people. It is, of course, the insignia of the Danish Order of the Elephant, which was popular in the eighteenth century.

This copy owned by Luxdorph contains his autograph on the front fly-leaf and a four-line epigraph in his hand on the back fly-leaf. Among his many accomplishments, Luxdorph was a distinguished collector of fine books. Another volume in this exhibition owned and autographed by Luxdorph is the first edition of the Danish translation of Hesiod (59).

1974—Gift of Peter A. Wick.

41
Ludvig Holberg (1684–1754)

Copenhagen & Leipzig:
Jacobus Preussius,
1741

Nicolai Klimii Iter Subterraneum

Holberg's first publications are in Danish. He was proud of his native language and defended its use, even in scholarly writings. In *Nicolai Klimii iter subterraneum*, however, he tries his hand at writing satirical narrative poetry in Latin. Because the Latin made it immediately available to readers from other countries, *Niels Klim* quickly became a favorite within the European community. It was for many years Holberg's most popular work and has been translated into many languages. Although it has not kept pace with the comedies, the interest in *Klim* is still evident. In 1960 a new English edition was issued by the University of Nebraska Press.

Niels Klim is written in the tradition of Jonathan Swift's *Gulliver's Travels*. The fantastic voyage underground takes Klim through adventures which offer Holberg ample opportunity to criticize contemporary society. Through exaggeration and acid paradox, Holberg satirizes religion, academia, and other institutions. But *Klim* is less pessimistic than *Gulliver*. While Swift attacks society, his real target is human nature. Holberg's Klim, though weak and silly, is still a human being with the capacity to develop his rational powers and moral awareness. Society is woven from the moral fabric of its individuals and improves when the moral fiber of each person is strengthened.

This first edition of *Klim*, published in both Denmark and Germany, contains seven engraved illustrations.

1941—Purchased with the Archibald Cary Coolidge (HC 1887) Fund.

42
Ludvig Holberg (1684–1754), Jens Baggesen (1764–1826), translator
Niels Klims Underjordiske Reise

Copenhagen:
Johan Frederik Schultz,
1789

The first Danish translation of *Niels Klim*, by Hans Hagerup, appeared in 1742. But it was not until almost fifty years later that *Klim* came to life for readers of Danish. In 1789 the talented poet Jens Baggesen produced an enduring Danish *Klim*. In this edition there are sixteen new engravings by Johan Frederik Clemens, fifteen of which are after Nicolai Abildgaard.

(a) 1856—Purchased with the Henry Ware Wales (HC 1838) Fund;
(b) 1984—Gift of Philip Hofer (HC 1921).

43
Ludvig Holberg (1684–1754) *Den Danske Comoedies Ligbegaengelse*

Copenhagen:
Johan Jørgen Hopffner,
1746

Inspired by the plays of Molière and the Italian *commedia dell' arte*, Holberg created a total of twenty-eight plays. These have proven to be the most enduring of his writings, and favorites like *Jeppe paa Bjerget* (*Jeppe of the Hill*), *Erasmus Montanus*, and *Den politiske Kandestøber* (*The Political Tinker*) are performed today in Denmark and abroad.

Holberg was brought into the theatre by invitation. In 1722 the first theatre for Danish scripts was to open in Copenhagen in the Lille Grønnegade under the leadership of actor-manager Montaigu. Recognizing the comic genius of the writer of *Peder Paars*, Montaigu invited Holberg to create new comedies for his troup. On 26 September 1722, Holberg's *The Political Tinker* opened, and the following year a collection of his comedies was published. In just over two years the inspired Holberg completed twenty-four comedies.

New restrictions forced Montaigu to close his theatre. For the scheduled closing on 25 February 1727, Holberg was asked to write a comedy. He created this one-act play, *Den danske Comoedies Ligbegaengelse* (*The Burial of Danish Comedy*), which was not published until twenty years later. Montaigu's theatre closed in 1728 and few plays were produced in Copenhagen for twenty years during the reign of Christian VI. But Danish comedy, of course, did not die. Holberg's satiric lamentation for the demise of Danish theatre, an occasional piece for 1727, is now read mostly for its historical interest.

1979—Gift of Joseph S. Stern, Jr. (HC 1940).

44
Christophe Barthélemy Fagan (1702–1755), B. J. Lodde (1706–1788), translator
Myndlingen

Copenhagen: H. K. M. Priv.
Bogtrykkerie,
1750

Before Holberg—with the exception of the wonderful Danish farce *Karrig Niding* (*Stingy Miser*) by Hieronymus Justesen Ranch (1539–1607)—only French, Italian, and a few German plays were performed in Copenhagen. In the 1720s, until the Lille Grønnegade closed in 1728, Holberg's comedies were the most popular form of dramatic entertainment. After 1748, when Frederick V opened the Royal Theatre in Kongens Nytorv, new scripts again were sought. Although Holberg wrote a few new comedies, many Danes again turned to French and German imports. They translated, adapted, and imitated the new foreign scripts.

Myndlingen, the Danish version of C. B. Fagan's musical comedy *La pupille*, is a good example of this kind of import. This first edition is of particular interest because of its engraved title vignette depicting the exterior of the new Royal Theatre.

1981—Purchased with the Amy Lowell Fund.

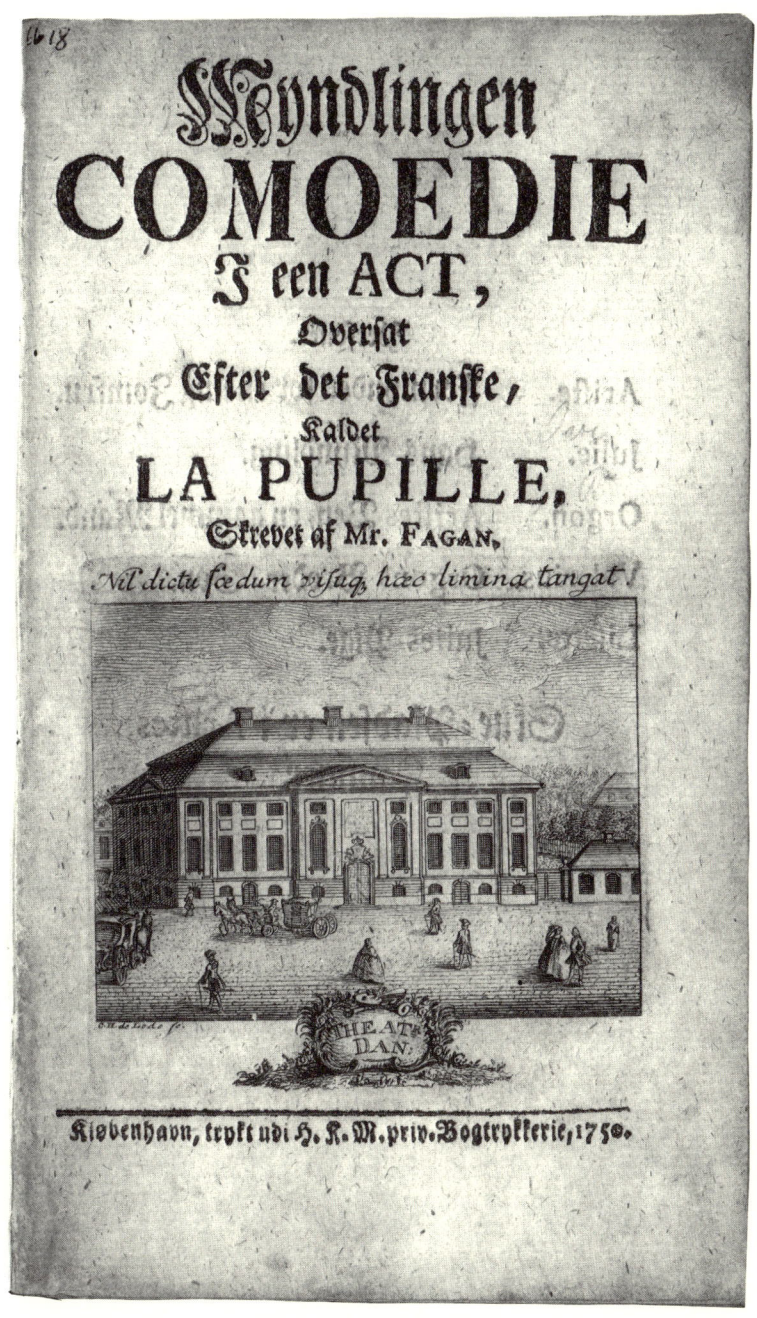

44   Fagan   *Myndlingen*   Copenhagen, 1750

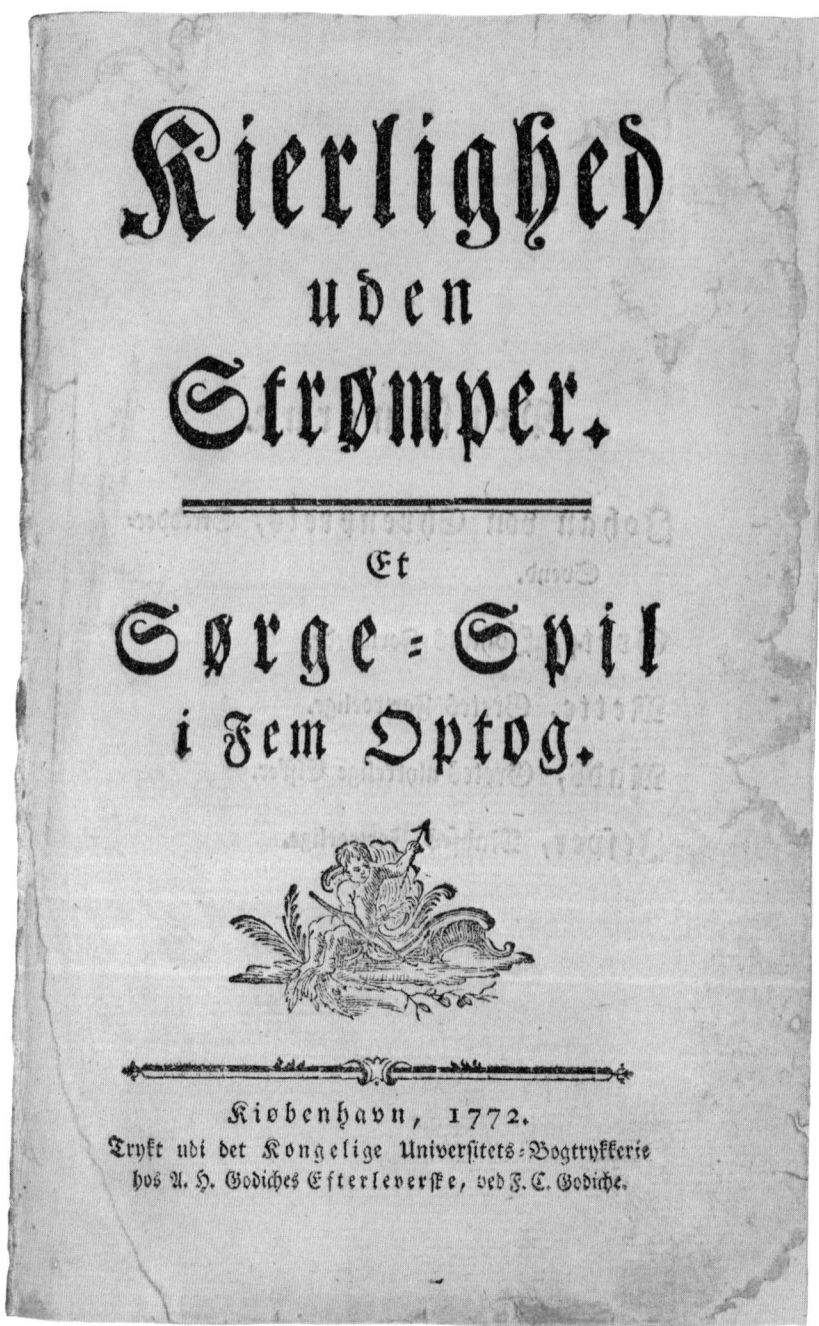

45   Wessel   *Kierlighed uden Strømper*   Copenhagen, 1772

45
Johan Herman Wessel (1742–1785) *Kierlighed uden Strømper*

Copenhagen:
A. H. Godiche; F. C. Godiche,
1772

Wessel was one of a new generation of young Norwegian writers settling in Copenhagen. He is known primarily for his play *Kierlighed uden Strømper* (*Love Without Stockings*) which carries on the spirit of Holberg. Just as Holberg satirizes in a number of his works the literary excesses of academic writing, Wessel mocks the exaggerated pathos and pretentious style of Danish imitators of French tragedy. When Johan Nordahl Brun won a prize for *Zarine*, a tragedy in the French manner, Wessel answered with his mock-heroic *Stockings*. This parody helped to put an end to the Danish taste for French imports. Wessel's play is still performed and is an immensely popular Danish classic.

1981—Purchased with the Amy Lowell Fund.

46
Christian V. Brunn (1794–1877) *Danske Theatercostumer* Vol. 1

Copenhagen,
1826

The Harvard Theatre Collection has recently acquired the four volumes of *Danske Theatercostumer* published between 1826 and 1829. These engraved and hand-colored plates provide invaluable information to the theatre historian studying costume design in the early nineteenth century. The volumes also provide a lively portfolio of some of the great actors of the time.

Among the roles portrayed are a couple of Holberg characters. This illustration from the first volume (1826) depicts Ludvig Vilhelm Lindgreen (1770–1842) as Jeppe. There were four notable Jeppes between 1722 and 1805 when Lindgreen inherited the role. Many think Lindgreen was the greatest.

This plate is by G. L. Lahde, who designed those in the first volume; the rest are by Bruun.

1985—Purchased with the Edwin Binney, 3rd (HC 1946) Fund.

47
Christian V. Brunn (1794–1877) *Danske Theatercostumer* Vol. 3

Copenhagen,
1828

This plate by Bruun is from the third volume (1828) of *Danske Theatercostumer*. It depicts another popular actor, Johan Christian Ryge, playing Olfux in Holberg's *Den Stundeløse* (*The Fussy Man*). Ryge, who lived from 1780 to 1842, was the fourth Olfux.

1985—Purchased with the Edwin Binney, 3rd (HC 1946) Fund.

T. W. inv.   I. F. C. Sculp.
Kiære Börn! jo meer ieg derpaa grunder,
Ieg da, faa Mary! feer der er heel andet under.

Hr. Lindgreens Costume som Ieppe
i Comedien Ieppe paa Bierget .

46   Bruun   *Danske Theatercostumer* Vol. 1   Copenhagen, 1826

From Classic to Romantic

The wit, the satire, the brilliance, the logic, and indeed the elegance of the best writers of the eighteenth century did not die with Holberg. Wessel's comic genius testifies to the contrary. Then, on his deathbed in 1785, Wessel wrote a final poem in which he welcomes the young poet Jens Baggesen to the company of Parnassus. The literary torch had been passed on. At the turn of the century fifteen years later, as he was about to leave Copenhagen for a life of voluntary exile, Baggesen formally bequeathed his literary muse to the twenty-one year old Adam Oehlenschläger. Although Baggesen was struggling against the new kind of poetry, he had the insight and grace to recognize in Oehlenschläger a significant talent.

Baggesen, Peder Andreas Heiberg, and Knud Lyhne Rahbek form the literary establishment of the end of the eighteenth century. But then there is the great lyric poet, Johannes Ewald, who stands alone, both classic and romantic. The purity of his lyrical voice and his exceptional skill with established verse forms mark the classic in Ewald. His love of old legends and the special passion of his inspiration turn him towards the Romanticism of the nineteenth century.

The center of the literary circle at the beginning of the nineteenth century and well into the years of Romanticism was the Rahbek household. The husband (professor, scholar, and sometime poet) and his wife Kamma (brilliant, witty, and cultured) attracted to their *salon* for more than fifty years the best minds of the time. Rahbek lived a long and busy life, and he witnessed profound changes in literary taste. But, never really understanding the new school of writing, he remained very much the keeper of the best of the classic.

48
Jens Baggesen (1764–1826) *Labyrinten*

Copenhagen:
Johan Frederik Schultz,
1792–93

Jens Baggesen was an accomplished poet and prose writer. In 1785 he gained immediate recognition with the publication of his first work, a versified collection of comic tales. In 1789 he translated *Niels Klim* (42). But his first important work is *Labyrinten*. Always the restless traveler, Baggesen was torn between his native Denmark and his intellectual attraction to Germany and France. It is fitting that one of his most important works describes a "journey through Germany, Switzerland, and France." *Labyrinten* contains a number of striking descriptive passages which seem almost realistic in their use of detail.

On display here is the first volume of this two-volume collection.

1982—Purchased with the Amy Lowell Fund.

49
Mindeblomster paa Faderens . . . og Sönnens . . . Grave

Copenhagen:
Andreas Seidelin,
1815

This collection of memorial poetry "for the grave of Captain W. H. F. Abrahamson and his son, Ludvig August" includes two contributions by Knud Lyhne Rahbek (1760–1830), "Gravsang" and "Mindetale." "Gravsang" is a good illustration of Rahbek's skill in versifying, and "Mindetale" shows his ability both as poet and critic.

This volume is opened to the engraved title page. The design reveals a tension between romantic motifs and the conventions of a classical formalism.

1947—Purchased with the Andrew Preston Peabody (HC 1826) Fund.

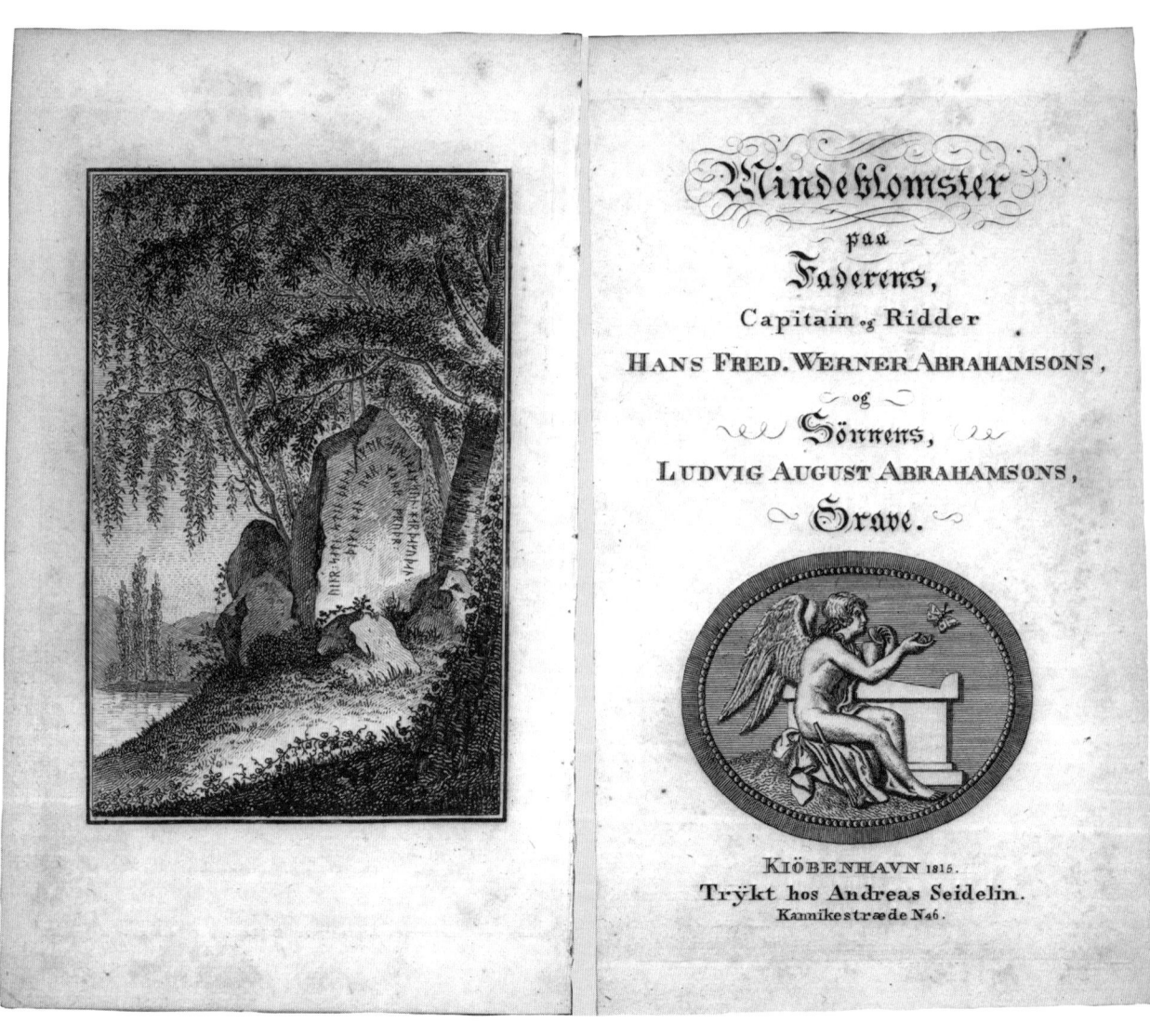

49   Rahbek et al.   *Mindeblomster*   Copenhagen, 1815

50
Johannes Ewald (1743–1781)   *Samtlige Skrifter* Vol. 1

Copenhagen:
Christian Gottlob Proft,
1780

Johannes Ewald lived a short but intense life. He left behind four volumes of some of the greatest poetry in Danish. A master of form, an elegant stylist, an innovator in metrical lines, Ewald also had the passion of a romantic soul. The tension between the two sides of Ewald's talents at times makes his lyrical poetry particularly exciting and moving. Other times, Ewald's lines may seem a little artificial to the modern ear.

The first volume of this four-volume collected edition of Ewald's poetry is open to a fine portrait designed and engraved by Johan Frederik Clemens. All four volumes are illustrated with numerous plates. The first group are by Clemens, after Nicolai Abildgaard. The remaining are engraved and designed by Daniel Chodowiecki.

1952—Gift of Dr. Elisabeth Deichmann.

51
Johannes Ewald (1743–1781)   *Samtlige Skrifter* Vol. 3

Copenhagen:
Christian Gottlob Proft,
1787

Johannes Ewald is arguably Denmark's greatest lyric poet. Although he may not be as well known internationally as Adam Oehlenschläger, Ewald is very much alive in Denmark today. It is fitting that the words of the Danish national anthem are by him. The song "Kong Christian" is from his last great work, *Fiskerne* (*The Fishermen*, 1779), a poetic tale which dramatizes the rugged life of Danes living on the coast. Ewald himself had lived for a while on the coast, in poverty and illness in the village of Rungsted on the Sound. This poem and others by Ewald have been translated into English by the American poet and scholar, Henry Wadsworth Longfellow.

The third volume of Ewald's collected writings is open to the text of the Danish national anthem, "King Christian Stood Beside the Lofty Mast."

1952—Gift of Dr. Elisabeth Deichmann.

52
Adam Oehlenschläger (1779–1850)   *Digte*

Copenhagen: Fr. Brummer;
Andreas Seidelin,
1803 [1802]

This famous edition of Oehlenschläger's first collection of verse marks the self-conscious beginning of the Romantic Movement in Denmark. In the fall of 1802 a young Norwegian philosopher, Henrik Steffens, gave a series of lectures in Copenhagen on German Romanticism. His passion for this new movement inspired the younger generation of Danish writers, including Oehlenschläger, to try a new kind of poetry. After Oehlenschläger first heard Steffens, the two reportedly met for a long and intense discussion of poetry. This meeting prompted Oehlenschläger to write his famous poem, *Guldhornene* (*The Golden Horns*), which symbolizes the beginning of the new Romantic School. A few months later, this and several other Oehlenschläger poems such as *Hakon Jarls Død* were published. Although the title page, engraved by Jeppe Sonne, is dated 1803, this first edition actually appeared in December 1802.

Earlier in 1802 the famous golden horns which Ole Worm (21) and Erik Pontoppidan (33) had described were stolen and melted down. The loss of these national treasures was shocking to Danes, including Oehlenschläger, who turns the story into a dramatic legend. He claims that the horns were a gift from the gods, symbolizing a heroic past, but were taken away again because modern generations have been unable to see more meaning in the horns than their material value. The mournful note

50 Ewald *Samtlige Skrifter* Vol. 1 Copenhagen, 1780

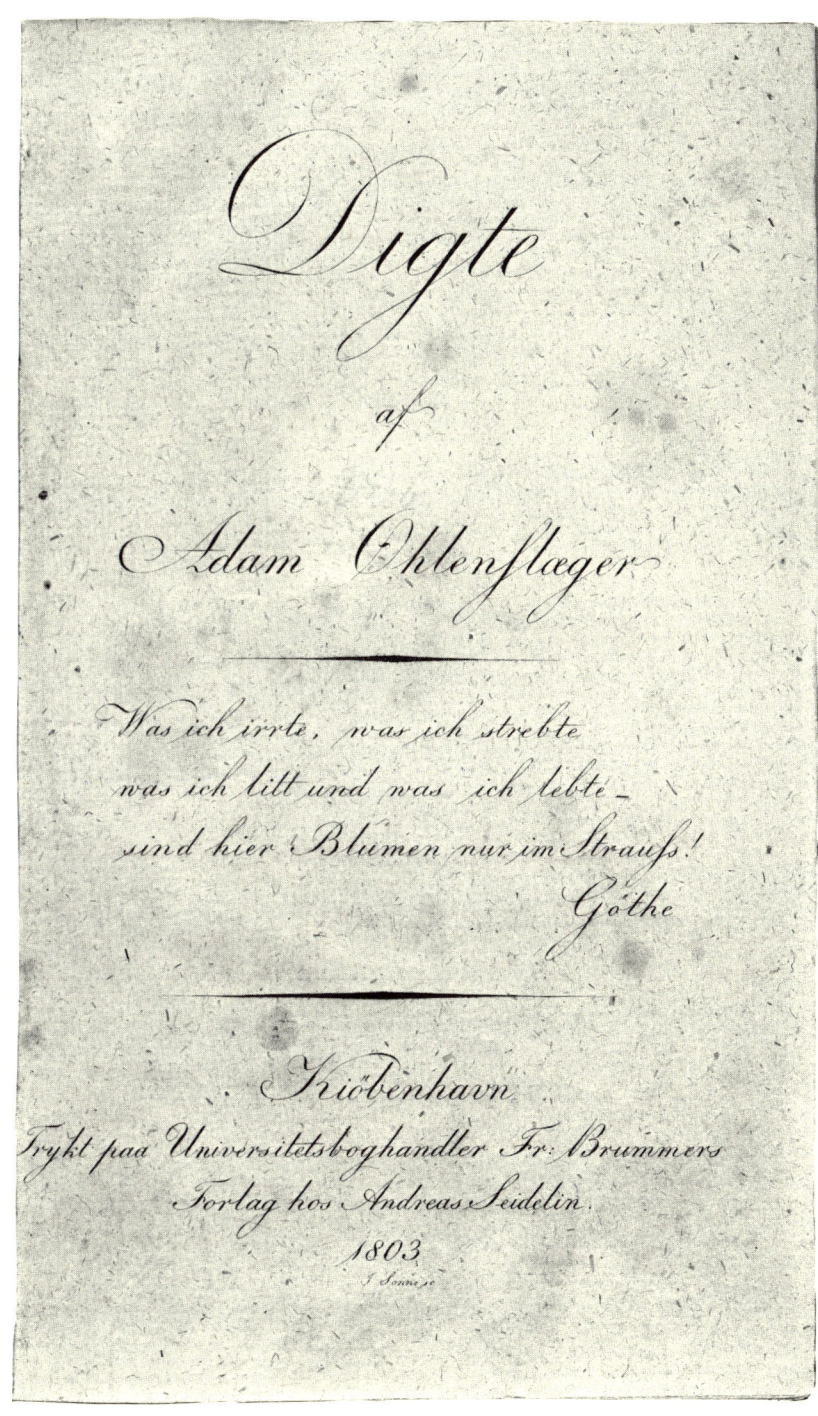

52   Oehlenschläger   *Digte*   Copenhagen, 1802

of the *Golden Horns* laments this loss, but there is also the hope that this song will help to arouse the dying spirit of the legendary past.

Digte and a number of other volumes in the exhibition were purchased for Harvard by Henry Wadsworth Longfellow in the fall of 1835, while studying and traveling in Scandinavia.

1835 — Purchased by Henry Wadsworth Longfellow.

53
Adam Oehlenschläger (1779 – 1850) et al.   *Siofna for Aaret* 1802

Copenhagen: G. Jacobsen, [1822]

This collection of poetry by Oehlenschläger and others includes several important poems. Oehlenschläger's *Kierlighed* (*Love*) is a central thematic piece for this volume dedicated to "Siofna," "Nordic goddess of love." The German expatriot, Adolph Wilhelm Schack von Staffeldt (1769– 1826), is also represented in this volume. The brooding Schack Staffeldt lived the life of the romantic poet, almost to the point of self parody, but he never achieved the greatness of Oehlenschläger.

1835 — Purchased by Henry Wadsworth Longfellow.

54
Adam Oehlenschläger (1779 – 1850)   *Alladdin* in *Poetiske Skrifter* Vol. 2

Copenhagen: J. H. Schubothe; Andreas Seidelin, 1805

After the 1802 *Digte* Oehlenschläger's next important work *Alladdin* appeared in this 1805 collection of *Poetiske Skrifter*. This dramatic poem, loosely based on the *Arabian Nights*, is one of the first Danish works to show freely the influence of Shakespeare. A blend of Eastern, Shakespearean, and Nordic elements, *Alladdin* achieves dramatic coherence, in part because of the unifying symbolic imagery of light and darkness.

1976 — Purchased with the George L. Lincoln (HC 1895) Fund.

55
Adam Oehlenschläger (1779 – 1850)   *Hakon Jarl hin Rige* in *Nordiske Digte*

Copenhagen: Andreas Seidelin, 1807

This third important Oehlenschläger collection includes *Hakon Jarl* and *Baldur*, historical dramas based on Norse legend. In these works Oehlenschläger carries out his project of *The Golden Horns*. He transforms ancient Nordic myth into living, contemporary verse. The calligraphic title page is by Sonne.

1835 — Purchased by Henry Wadsworth Longfellow.

56
Bernard Severin Ingemann (1789–1862) *De Sorte Riddere*

Copenhagen: Boas Brünnich,
1814

A contemporary of Oehlenschläger, Ingemann can readily be classified a "Romantic." But he is closer to Ludwig Tieck than to Goethe or A. W. Schlegel. This "romantic epic in nine songs," *De sorte Riddere* (*The Black Knights*), is an allegorical tale derived more from medieval and early Renaissance courtly legends than from the Old Norse tales Oehlenschläger preferred. Ingemann was deeply influenced, as were many of his Scandinavian and German contemporaries, by the novels of Sir Walter Scott. Ingemann's poetry and prose enjoyed wide popularity during his lifetime. He was occasionally criticized, however, for his fantastic abstractions.

1984—Purchased with the Amy Lowell Fund.

57
Christian Winther (1796–1876) *Hjortens Flugt*

Copenhagen: C. A. Reitzel;
Bianco Luno
1856

Oehlenschläger, Ingemann, and Schack Staffeldt are pioneering Romantic poets in early nineteenth-century Denmark. Christian Winther belongs to a younger generation of Romantics. He published his first poems long after Oehlenschläger's ground-breaking *Digte*, at a time when the Romantic style no longer shocked. Winther's writings were not popular at first, but this cycle of romances set in fifteenth-century Zealand, *Hjortens Flugt* (*Flight of the Stag*), was exceedingly popular when it was first published. And it remained popular throughout the nineteenth century, going through many editions.

Like Ingemann, Winther uses late medieval settings; but his are more "realistic," the passion more concrete. He is less tempted by the idealistic fantasies of writers of the early nineteenth century.

1980—Purchased with the Amy Lowell Fund.

59   Hesiod   *Hesiodus Fordansket oc udi Rijm Offversatt*   Copenhagen, 1670

Translations into Danish

The Danish language may be traced to its earliest Proto-Scandinavian form. Many scholars now agree that the oldest runic inscriptions are from Denmark, where Rune Danish thrived. And yet Denmark was never large and powerful enough to create a major tongue of Europe. The kingdom of Denmark has been a scattered and changing group of islands and peninsulas near the edge of the European continent. Danish writers have had to struggle to free themselves from the dominance of other tongues. An important part of Danish cultural history is the changing relationship of Danish to other languages and the history of translations in Denmark, both into and from Danish. Early writers of Danish often felt they had to justify and defend the use of the vernacular instead of the more acceptable Latin. Works were frequently written first in Latin and later translated into Danish. The first important work of Danish literature, Saxo's *Chronicle*, is in Latin and was not fully translated into Danish until about four centuries later. It was not until Holberg received international recognition that Danish began to be fully accepted as the first language of literary Denmark.

After Holberg, most Danish writers have continued to be fluent in more than one tongue and have often experimented with other languages. For example Baggesen, the poet who created a Danish *Niels Klim*, occasionally preferred to write in German. Hans Christian Andersen, the great teller of Danish tales, wrote his autobiography first in German. Isak Dinesen created both English and Danish versions of her tales. But with the international significance of Holberg, Andersen, Kierkegaard, and Dinesen, no one today can doubt the greatness of Danish literature and the Danish tongue.

This selection of translations from the Houghton Danish collection provides an overview of some of the work being done in Danish translations between the mid-seventeenth century and the beginning of the nineteenth century.

58
Snorri Sturlason (1178–1241), Peder Johan Resen (1625–1688) translator   *Edda*

Copenhagen:
Henricus Gödianus,
1665

This remarkable book is the first Icelandic-Danish-Latin text of Snorri Sturlason's *Edda*. In presenting all three languages in parallel translation, Resen made certain that all needs were met. The linguist could compare the three versions; the non-Scandinavian could read the Latin; and the Dane with shaky Latin and little Icelandic could rely on the Danish version. And, of course, the original Icelandic is provided for the scholar.

With the assistance of Stefán Ólafsson, the Latin translation of the first part of the *Edda* (to the sixty-eighth tale) is by Magnús Ólafsson, who edited the Icelandic text from the *Codex Wormianus*. The remaining translations are by Thormod Torfaeus, and the overall editing is by Peder Resen.

1895 — Gift of Francis B. Hayes (HC 1839).

59
Hesiod (ca. 800 B.C.?), Henrik Thomaesøn Gerner (1629–1700) translator
Hesiodus Fordansket oc udi Rijm Offversatt

Copenhagen: Daniel Eichhorn;
Christian Cassubens
& Christian Gertsen,
1670

During the eighteenth century, a number of poets and scholars translated the classics into Danish. They hoped to bring to Denmark as many Greek and Latin texts as possible, to bring Denmark into closer contact with classical civilizations. Danish historians were also interested in late Roman texts which discuss the relationship between Rome and the early migration of Nordic tribes. For example, in 1746 Holberg translated the historian Herodian, who lived after 238 A.D.

On display here is a translation of selected verse by a much earlier poet, Hesiod. This volume is from Luxdorph's library and is autographed by him. With his *Carmina* (40), this *Hesiod* is a good example of fine eighteenth-century bookbinding.

1965 — Purchased with the George L. Lincoln (HC 1895) Fund.

60

Miguel de Cervantes (1547–1616), Charlotte Dorothea Biehl (1731–1788) translator   *Den Sindrige Herremands Don Quixote af Mancha Levnet og Bedrifter*

Copenhagen: Gyldendal,
1776–1777

Denmark is not known for its eighteenth-century prose novels. Both *Peder Paars* and *Niels Klim* are versified forms of satirical fiction. The only novelist of note during this period is Charlotte Dorothea Biehl. Her *Moralske Fortaellinger* (*Moral Tales*, 1781–82) are, for the most part, only imitations of English and French models.

Biehl's outstanding contribution to Danish literature is her four-volume translation of *Don Quixote*. On display here is the first volume, opened to the title page. The frontispiece is an engraved portrait of Cervantes by Meno Haas. The text illustrations throughout this edition are engraved by Meno Haas' brother, Georg, and by J. G. Preisler, after the French illustrations of Charles Coypel.

1942 — Gift of Philip Hofer (HC 1921).

61

William Shakespeare (1564–1616), Johannes Boye (1756–1830) translator *Hamlet, Prinz af Dannemark*

Copenhagen: M. Hallager,
1777

In 1777 *Hamlet* was translated into Danish by Johannes Boye. As the plot is based on the Danish legend preserved by Saxo, it is fitting that *Hamlet* was the first Shakespeare to appear in Danish.

1970 — Purchased with the Walter Wehle Naumberg (HC 1889) Fund.

62

Ossian (James Macpherson 1736–1796), Steen Steensen Blicher (1782–1848) translator   *Ossians Digte*

Copenhagen:
Reitzel; Andreas Seidelin,
1807–1809

Blicher, the great nineteenth-century writer of short stories and poetry, began his writing career with this translation of Ossian. In the late eighteenth century, Macpherson's Ossian had been popular throughout Europe and was a central text in the development of romanticism and nationalism in literature.

For this first edition Blicher provides a lengthy "scholarly preface" in which he describes the significance of Ossian and argues for the validity of the text. At this time it had not yet been firmly established that Ossian was only Macpherson's creation. Many still assumed with Blicher that Ossian was indeed a genuine ancient Scottish bard. The eminently sensible Dr. Johnson, however, was one of the more probing skeptics. In this preface Blicher dismisses, with youthful and romantic enthusiasm, the arguments of Dr. Johnson point by point.

Thirty years later, near the end of his career, Blicher chose a very different translation project, Oliver Goldsmith's *Vicar of Wakefield* (*Praesten i Wakefield*, 1837). This interest in Goldsmith is appropriate for the mature Blicher, a provincial vicar in Jutland and a writer of richly detailed realistic prose. With this choice of provincial Wakefield over the romantic

HAMLET,

PRINZ AF DANNEMARK.

TRAGOEDIE

AF

SHAKESPEAR.

OVERSAT AF ENGELSK.

KIÖBENHAVN,
TRYKT HOS M. HALLAGER.
1777.

61 Shakespeare *Hamlet, Prinz af Dannemark* Copenhagen, 1777

caves of Fingal, Blicher shows how his taste changed over a period of thirty years. He developed into a great prose fiction writer closer to the sensible and concrete world of Dr. Johnson and Oliver Goldsmith than he might originally have ever imagined possible.

1970—Purchased with the George L. Lincoln (HC 1895) Fund.

63
Saxo Grammaticus (ca. 1150–ca. 1220), N. F. S. Grundtvig (1783–1872) translator   *Danmarks Krønike af Saxo Grammaticus Fordansket*

Copenhagen:
Krønikens Danske & Norske
Venner; Schultz,
1818

Between 1813 and 1822 N. F. S. Grundtvig produced three important translations of early texts: Saxo's *Chronicle*, Snorri Sturlason *Edda*, and the Anglo-Saxon epic *Beowulf*. In these volumes, with a contemporary colloquial touch, Grundtvig brings the medieval world back to life for his nineteenth-century readers. In doing so he takes a few liberties with the original texts—a license for which he sometimes is criticized.

N. F. S. Grundtvig's voice was strong and persuasive. He spoke out against the "decadent liberties" of eighteenth-century literature and turned for inspiration to Old Norse and Germanic literature and the stories of the Bible. In 1827 he wrote "I serve the spirit of the Bible, of History, and of the North." A writer of hymns and inspirational essays, Grundtvig is also an important theologian. In his spiritual writings, his goal was the union of the Christian faith and the mystical elements of Old Norse mythology. This volume and the Snorri *Edda* are published for "the man in the street" by "the Chronicle's Danish and Norwegian Friends."

1835—Purchased by Henry Wadsworth Longfellow.

The Nineteenth Century

The nineteenth century was an exciting period for Danish literature. Oehlenschläger led the Romantic Movement with his fine lyric voice. Blicher showed how Danish prose could be subtle, realistic, and contemporary. Rahbek, J. L. Heiberg, and, later in the century, Georg Brandes, formed influential literary circles which inspired some of Denmark's greatest writers. Heiberg and his actress wife, Johanne Luise Heiberg, helped to make theatre more realistic and appealing to the ordinary middle classes. Jacobsen wrote his famous naturalistic novels. Ørsted discovered the principle of electromagnetism. And, once again, Denmark emerged as an international literary and philosophical force with the achievements of the two great intellects, Hans Christian Andersen and Søren Kierkegaard.

Hans Christian Andersen is known and cherished by child and adult throughout the world. Everyone knows the stories of *The Ugly Duckling*, *The Princess and the Pea*, and *The Emperor's New Clothes*. It would be difficult to list all the editions and translations of his tales. But Andersen's achievements are not limited to his many tales; he is also famous in Denmark for his novels, plays, and brilliant travelogues.

Andersen's contemporary, Søren Kierkegaard, is at least as well known throughout the world. With the revival of interest in the philosophy of Existentialism, Kierkegaard is a favorite among philosophy students today. He takes a prominent place among the great names of philosophy, from Plato to Wittgenstein.

The Houghton Library is fortunate to have a nearly complete collection of first editions of Kierkegaard. Many important volumes could be selected to represent him; we have had to limit the choice to only two.

64
Steen Steensen Blicher (1782–1848) et al.   *Bautastene*

Odense: S. Hempel,
1823

This collection of commemorative poetry, published in Odense and dedicated to the great writers of Denmark's past, is edited by Blicher. Most of the poems are by Blicher himself, but the poetry of several others is also represented, including Oehlenschläger, Ingemann, and N. S. F. Grundtvig. The writers memorialized include Saxo, Brahe, Holberg, Huitfeldt, and Ewald. The lithographed title page depicts a pyramid of memorial stones, each inscribed with the name of a great Danish author, and is signed by "CHBH."

1971 — Purchased with the George L. Lincoln (HC 1895) Fund.

65
Steen Steensen Blicher (1782–1848)   *Samlede Digte* Vol. 1

Copenhagen: C. Steen;
Bianco Luno & Schneider,
1835

Blicher, whose first publication is his translation of Ossian (62), was known initially as a poet. Although more famous as a writer of prose, he is also cherished today for a few favorite poems. Several have become popular songs. Blicher's poetry was first collected in 1835–36, in two volumes. The Houghton copy, which has the original wrappers and spine strips, is open in this exhibition to the frontispiece portrait of Blicher by F. W. Goedsche.

1973 — Purchased with the Amy Lowell Fund.

64   Blicher et al.   *Bautastene*   Odense, 1823

66
Steen Steensen Blicher (1782–1848)   *En Landsbydegns Dagbog* in *Samlede Noveller* Vol. 1

Copenhagen: C. Steen;
Bianco Luno & Schneider,
1833

It was not until Blicher was nearly forty years old that he found his true literary form, the short story. His stories are known for the way they capture the local color of the Jutland moors and sanddowns where he lived. Occasionally Blicher makes his descriptions of Jutland even more realistic by writing in the dialect of his native Viborg. In 1824, soon after becoming a parish priest in Jutland, he wrote his famous *En Lands-bydegns Dagbog* (*Journal of a Country Footman*). One of the important characters, Sophie, is based on the same seventeenth-century figure, Marie Grubbe, whom Jens Peter Jacobsen made famous fifty-two years later in his novel *Fru Marie Grubbe* (84).

Blicher's tales were first collected in five volumes, with a sixth "supplement," between 1833 and 1846. The first volume (1833) is open in this exhibition to his *En Landsbydegns Dagbog*.

1971 — Purchased with the Duplicate Fund.

67
Steen Steensen Blicher (1782–1848) et al.   *Nordlyset: Et Maanedsskrivt* Vol. 1

Randers: S. Elmenhoff,
1827

A number of important Danish writers have been responsible for literary journals. Bording, Rahbek, J. L. Heiberg, and Blicher are among the more famous literary editors. With J. M. Elmenhoff, Blicher published in Randers the Jutland periodical *Nordlyset* between January 1827 and December 1829. In all there are twelve volumes, with four numbers for each of the three years. Most of the literary contributions are by Blicher himself, but a few other Jutish writers such as Ole Bork are represented. Ole Bork was also a parish priest from Blicher's district and signed his name "B," as did Blicher.

1971 — Purchased with the Amy Lowell Fund.

68
Hans Christian Ørsted (1777–1851)   *Experimenta circa Effectum Conflictus Electrici in Acum Magneticam*

Copenhagen: Schultz,
1820

The talented Ørsted brothers, Hans Christian and Anders Sandøe, were central figures in nineteenth-century Denmark. Hans Christian Andersen celebrates the achievements of the two Ørsteds in his tale *De to Brødre* (*The Two Brothers*). Anders was a famous jurist whose writings in legal philosophy helped to free jurisprudence from rationalist abstractions and absolutes. Inspired by Kant, A. S. Ørsted's influence brought more flexibility to Danish law. Anders married the talented sister of Adam Oehlenschläger.

Hans Christian Ørsted is now the more famous of the two brothers. In April 1820, while performing an experiment during an evening lecture at the University of Copenhagen, he discovered the phenomenon of electromagnetism. Ørsted immediately published a paper describing this fundamental force of nature. To reach the community of world scientists, he wrote in Latin. In 1932, to honor Ørsted's achievements, physicists formally adopted the term "oersted," replacing "gauss" as the unit of magnetic-field strength.

Ørsted went on to write a number of important philosophical works on natural philosophy and empiricism. Hans Christian Andersen and Søren Kierkegaard both admit to having been influenced by the writings of Ørsted.

1986 — Lent by David P. Wheatland (HC 1922).

69
Johan Ludvig Heiberg (1791–1860) et. al.   *Kjøbenhavns Flyvende Post*

Copenhagen:
Jens Hostrup Schultz,
1828

The son of two authors, Peter Andreas Heiberg and Thomasine Buntzen (Countess Gyllembourg), Johan Ludvig Heiberg was blessed with a strong intellectual heritage. He also lived as a youth for two years with the Rahbeks. The women in Heiberg's life were particularly influential. His mother, probably a more talented writer than his father, was a teller of tales which Heiberg published for her anonymously in his periodical *Kjøbenhavns flyvende Post*. Fru Rahbek, the superior wit of the Rahbek household, brought sparkle to her husband's literary circle. And Johan Ludvig went on to marry Johanne Luise, the most famous actress in Danish stage history. Fru Heiberg also showed some talent as an author. She wrote several popular vaudevilles and an autobiographical memoir (71). Hans Christian Andersen reports that it was Fru Heiberg who had the most encouraging words for him as a writer; in gratitude, he dedicated to her his 1842 booklet of tales.

The Heibergs, the Rahbeks, the Ørsteds, the Oehlenschlägers, Frederik Paludan-Müller, Hans Christian Andersen, and Søren Kierkegaard all knew each other. It is impossible to discuss nineteenth-century Danish literature without noting the interaction of the members of the Heiberg circle.

In 1827 Heiberg began publishing his *Kjøbenhavns flyvende Post*, issued in four-page numbers, 104 per year. The run was brief, from 1827 to the end of 1828, and then again in 1830. For four more years from 1834 to 1837, it was revived under the title *Interimsblade*.

Not only did Heiberg publish his mother's tales and his own essays, but he also published an anonymous essay by young Kierkegaard on the position of women in Danish society and introduced Hans Christian Andersen to the Copenhagen literary scene. In Number 90 of the *Post* (14 November 1828), Andersen presented the first part of his *Fodreise fra Holmens Canal til Øst-Pynten af Amager i Aaren 1828 og 1829 (Journey by Foot from Holm Canal to the East Point of Amager in the Years 1828 and 1829)*. The rest of this work was published in subsequent issues. *Fodreise* marked a turning point in the career of the young Andersen. For the first time he was taken seriously and was able to proceed in 1829 with its full publication in one volume. Then in 1830 Andersen's first real tale appeared in a new collection of his writings (73).

In this exhibition the 1828 volume is opened to Number 90, the first part of Andersen's *Fodreise*.

1952—Gift of Dr. Elisabeth Deichmann.

70
Johan Ludvig Heiberg (1791–1860)   *Om Vaudevillen*

Copenhagen:
Jens Hostrup Schultz,
1826

Another important contribution of Heiberg to Danish literature is his influential essay *Om Vaudevillen*, which first appeared in 1826. With this essay Heiberg argued the significance of the new form of musical drama, the vaudeville. He defended vaudeville as a serious form of comedy and argued that it was not to be confused with opera bouffe and other dramatic genres. Heiberg's own best-known play *Elverhøj* (1828) is an example of the vaudeville form he defended. Combining ballet, music, and the story of Christian IV, *Elverhøj* has remained popular on the Danish stage and is still produced today.

The Houghton copy of *Om Vaudevillen* has its original cream wrappers preserved.

1982—Purchased with the Amy Lowell Fund.

1828. № 90.

Kjøbenhavns flyvende Post.

Fredagen den 14de November.

Redigeret af J. L. Heiberg. Udgiven af Ferdinand Printzlau.

Pröver

af

et Skrift, betitlet:

"Fodreise fra Holmens Canal til Øst-Pynten af Amager i Aarene 1828 og 1829, udgiven af H. C. Andersen."*)

I.

Første Capitel.

(Hvorledes Satan faaer Magt over Forfatteren. — Synd-floden No. 2, en Mythe.)

Nytaars-Aften 1828 sad jeg ganske ene paa mit lille Værelse og saae ud over de sneebedækte Tage paa alle Nabohusene; da foer den onde Aand, som man kalder Satan, ind i mig, og indblæste mig den syndige Tanke at blive Forfatter. — Hvorfor han ellers saaledes gaaer paa Jagt efter os arme Mennesker, vil følgende Mythe lære; man kan kalde den:
Syndfloden Nr. 2.

— Og Gud Herren sagde til Noah og hans Slægt: "jeg opretter min Pagt med Eder, at her-

*) Dette humoristiske Skrift af en ung Digter, der allerede ved adskillige lyriske Smaastykker har vidst at gjøre sig værdig til Publicums Deeltagelse, vil udkomme i Slutningen af næste Maaned. Subscriptionsplaner vil om faa Dage blive udstædte. Red. Anm.

efter skal ikke alt Kjød ødelægges af Flodens Vande; og der skal ikke komme Flod herefter at fordærve Jorden!" Da hvælvede Regnbuen sig som et Pagtens Tegn, og Noah stolede paa Jehova. Men i Dybet hørte Satan Herrens Ord, og skar Tænder i sin Vrede; thi ogsaa den Herre Gud har sine Fiender, og den største kaldes: Satan. Gjerne vilde han kjæmpe imod Herrens Naade, men det var ham haardt at stampe imod Braadden; Have og Søer, Floder og Bække havde hørt den Herre Jehovas Ord, og vare, som Skyerne, hans Villie underdanige. Da grundede Satan i tre tusinde Aar, og paa det fjerde sprang han op og raabte: "Funtus! jeg har det! — Fra Menneskene selv skal det Onde udgaae; en ny Vandflod skal over-skylle Verden, skjøndt han sagde: der skal ikke komme Flod herefter at fordærve Jorden." Og Satan kaldte paa alle sine Vasaller og sagde: "Messieurs! drager ud over den hele Verden og forfø-rer Adams Sønner til at blive slette Skribenter, fra dem selv skal da Vandfloden udgaae, der for-dærver Jorden. Jeg vil gjøre mit, gjøre I nu Eders." Og de gjorde som han sagde, og strax flød der Vand i Øst og i Vest, i Syd og i Nord; det strømmer endnu og vil fordærve Jorden.

Enhver maa troe, at jeg af alle Kræfter stræbte imod, men Kjødet er skrøbeligt; den Onde havde nu engang sat sig fast i Kroppen, og jeg maatte

71
Joanne Luise Heiberg (1812–1890)   *Et Liv Gjenoplevet i Erindringen*

Copenhagen: Gyldendal,
1891–92

Fru Heiberg also wrote vaudevilles such as *En Søndag-paa Amager* (*A Sunday at Amager*, 1848) and *En Sommeraften* (*A Summer Evening*, 1853). Her most successful work, though, is her autobiography, *Et Liv gjenoplevet i Erindringen* (*A Life Relived in Memory*), which was not published until 1891–92, after her death in 1890. For theatre historians, Andersen and Kierkegaard scholars, and anyone studying the Heiberg circle, these memoirs are an invaluable source of information.

Kierkegaard's earlier work, *Krisen og en Krise i en Skuespillerindes Liv* (*The Crisis and a Crisis in the Life of an Actress*, 1848), is based on his own acquaintance with the life of Johanne Luise Heiberg.

This first edition of *Et Liv* is open to a portrait of Fru Heiberg and to a passage in which she describes a visit to the island of Ven, where Tycho Brahe built his observatories at the end of the sixteenth century.

1918—Gift of Evert Jansen Wendell (HC 1882).

72
Hans Christian Andersen (1805–1875)   *Ungdoms-Forsøg*

Copenhagen:
P. T. Schovelin; E. M. Cohen,
1827

Born of poor parents in Odense, Andersen left home at fourteen to seek his fortune in Copenhagen. He had hoped to become an actor, but only managed a few walk-on roles. His first literary effort was a little tragedy, *Alfsol*, which he sent to Jonas Collin of the Royal Theatre. Although but an imitative and naive work, *Alfsol* demonstrated enough promise to catch the attention of Collin. He arranged for funds from Frederik VI to send Andersen off for some schooling.

While beginning his studies Andersen continued to push his first compositions. He found a handful of subscribers to support the publication of *Alfsol* and a story, *Gjenfaerdet ved Palnatokes Grav* (*The Ghost at Palnatoke's Grave*). In 1822 a hundred copies of these *Ungdoms-Forsøg* (*Youthful Efforts*) were published by the widow of E. M. Cohen. Andersen used a pseudonym for this publication, Villiam Christian Walter: "Villiam" for Shakespeare, "Christian" for his own name, and "Walter" for Sir Walter Scott.

Only seventeen of these were sold—all to Andersen himself. A few years later, the publisher P. T. Schovelin bought the remaining eighty-three and released them in 1827 under a new title page. This reissue also failed to sell, and the copies ended up, so the story goes, in the hands of a fishmonger, for scrap paper.

Both the 1822 and the 1827 issues of this first work are very rare. Only two or three of the 1827 issue are known to have survived.

1986—Gift of the Friends of the Harvard College Library.

73
Hans Christian Andersen (1805–1875)   *Dödningen* in *Digte*

Copenhagen: Author's Press;
C. H. Robert,
1830 [1829]

Andersen's first literary success was the publication of his *Fodreise* in *Kjøbenhavns flyvende Post* (69). When this piece was released in one volume in 1829, it was reviewed favorably by Heiberg and finally brought attention to the young Andersen. A few months later, at the end of the year, he published his first "eventyr," the term which he used for the rest of his career to refer to the special form of folk tale which he made so famous. The "eventyr" appears at the end of this volume of poetry and bears the title *Dødningen, et fyensk Folke-eventyr* (*The Spectre, a Fynish*

Folk Tale). Andersen wrote later that this tale was based on a story he had heard as a child. A few years later he reworked it, under the title "The Traveling Companion," to give it the "true spirit" of his "eventyr."

In 1835 Andersen published his first collection of tales. This booklet was sixty-one pages long and contained five tales, including the famous *The Princess and the Pea*.

1971 — Purchased with the Amy Lowell Fund.

74
Hans Christian Andersen (1805 – 1875) *Mit Livs Eventyr* in *Samlede Skrifter* Vol. 21/22

Copenhagen: C. A. Reitzel; Bianco Luno, 1855

In 1847 Andersen wrote in German and published in Leipzig the tale of his own life. Seven years later he released the Danish version of this autobiography, *Mit Livs Eventyr*, published as Volume 21/22 of his collected works *Samlede Skrifter*. This collected edition was released in twenty-eight volumes, two to a book, between 1853 and 1868. After Andersen died in 1873, five more volumes of his works were published, along with a final supplementary volume. In this exhibition Volume 21/22 is opened to the title page, with a frontispiece portrait of Andersen.

1873 — Purchased with the Subscription Fund.

75
Hans Christian Andersen (1805 – 1875) *Ugedagene* in *Nye Eventyr og Historier* Vol. 5

Copenhagen: C. A. Reitzel; Thiele, 1874

Throughout his lifetime Andersen published his famous tales. The first collection, *Eventyr*, was released in 1835. Eight years later *Nye Eventyr* was published, a collection that brought him international fame. It was with this collection that the critical world hailed the "eventyr" as a new genre. Andersen's form of tale is, of course, not entirely original but is derived from ancient fables and folk tales. It was Andersen, however, who helped to give the old folk genres the literary respectability they now enjoy.

After *Samlede Skrifter* was released between 1853 and 1868, a third collection of tales was published in five volumes, *Nye Eventyr og Historier* (1870 – 74). This collection contains some previously published tales and others which had never before been released. One of his last tales *Ugedagene* (*The Days of the Week*) appears in the final volume. This short, ironic tale imagines what might happen if all the days of the week got together for dinner.

The fifth volume of this collection is opened to *Ugedagene*. The original illustration is by Lorenz Frølich.

1980 — Purchased with the Amy Lowell Fund.

76
Hans Christian Andersen (1805 – 1875) [Autograph Manuscript for *Ugedagene*]

[No place: no date]

The Houghton Library owns the original manuscript to *Ugedagene*. No date or place is recorded on this single-sheet manuscript. The sheet is folded in half to create two leaves or four pages, and the final page is signed by Andersen.

1925 — Bequest of Amy Lowell.

I.W.Tegner lith.   I.W.Tegner & Kittendorff lith. Inst.

74   Andersen   *Samlede Skrifter* Vol. 21/22   Copenhagen, 1855

Ugedagene.

Vignet til Februar.

Uge=Dagene vilde ogsaa engang slaae sig løs, komme sammen og holde Gilde. Hver Dag var iøvrigt saa optaget at de Aaret rundt ikke havde Fritid at raade over; de maatte have en apart heel Dag, men den havde de da ogsaa hvert fjerde Aar: Skuddagen, der lægges i Februar for at bringe Orden i Tidsreg= :ningen.

Paa Skuddagen vilde de altsaa kom =me sammen til Gilde og da ~~de~~ Februar er Fastelavns Maaned, vilde de komme Carnevalsklædte efter hvers Fornemmelse og Bestemmelse, spise godt, drikke godt holde Taler og sige hinanden Behage= :ligheder og Ubehageligheder i ugeneert Kammeratskab. Oldtidens Helte i Nor =den kastede hinanden, ved Maaltiderne de afgnavede Kjødbeen i Hovedet, Uge= :dagene vilde derimod dænge hinanden over med Mundgodt af Brandere og skarpagtige Vittigheder som de kunne falde i uskyldige Fastelavns Løier.

Saa var det Skuddag, og saa kom de sammen. Søndag, Formand for Ugedagene, traadte op i sort Silkekappe; fromme Mennesker vilde tro at han var præsteklædt til at

77

Hans Christian Andersen (1805–1875)   [Two Autograph Letters to Henry Wadsworth Longfellow]

Copenhagen: 24 March 1868;
Copenhagen: July 1871

The Houghton Library also owns two autograph letters from Andersen to Henry Wadsworth Longfellow. The earlier (24 March 1868) is in Danish and is mailed from Copenhagen. The second is dated "July 1871," just four years before his death. It is written in English and mailed from Copenhagen. In this letter, Andersen refers to one of his last works, *Lykke Peer*, published in 1870.

1976—Gift of the Trustees of Henry Wadsworth Longfellow.

78

Søren Kierkegaard (1813–1855)   *Enten-Eller*

Copenhagen: C. A. Reitzel;
Bianco Luno,
1843

While Kierkegaard is known primarily for his philosophy, he is also an accomplished literary artist. His first major work, and in many ways his most accessible, is the great *Enten-Eller* (*Either/Or*). Constructed in an original, mixed literary style, reminiscent in places of the eighteenth-century epistolary novel, *Enten-Eller* displays a finely crafted sense of form. The organization of the work is complex. It is written in several parts, with numerous pseudonymous authors apparently responsible for the different collections of papers, letters, and diaries. It seems at first to be only a loosely structured philosophical novel. But these disparate materials define two contrasting ways of life, the "either/or" of the title. On the one hand there is the life of the aesthetic person who is seduced by the world of the senses. And on the other hand there is the life of the ethical person who lives strictly according to an ethical code. For Kierkegaard the best way of life is neither. The "either/or" should instead be synthesized and transcended to a higher, religious life.

This 1843 first edition of only 525 copies was published at the author's own expense in two parts in one volume.

Old gift.

79

Søren Kierkegaard (1813–1855)   *Stadier paa Livets Vei*

Copenhagen: C. A. Reitzel;
Bianco Luno,
1845

After publishing *Enten-Eller*, Kierkegaard worked quickly and within the space of four years had completed most of his greatest works. *Stadier paa Livets Vei* (*Stages on Life's Way*) is another important philosophical work which exhibits outstanding literary artistry. It, too, is written in the form of a novel, and it, too, depicts three ways of life.

One of the most striking sections of this work, a beautifully written defense of the Danish language, appears near the end. This passionate statement is clearly Kierkegaard's own testimony and helps to explain the significance of his contribution to Danish literature. *Stadier* is open to this passage, which I translate in part: "I am fortunate to be bound to my mother tongue, bound as few are, bound as Adam to Eve, as there is no other woman, bound because I have not been able to learn another language and thus have not stood proud and haughty with this knowledge. I am also glad to be bound to a mother tongue and its inner riches, its originality expanding the soul, ringing sweetly in the ear, a mother tongue that does not groan under a burden of difficult thought . . . ." Kierkegaard, poet and master of the Danish tongue, makes the language "ring sweetly" with "difficult thought"!

This copy has the original stiffened blue wrappers preserved.

1953—Gift of Curt H. Reisinger (HC 1912).

Enten — Eller.

Et Livs-Fragment

udgivet

af

Victor Eremita.

Første Deel

indeholdende A.'s Papirer.

Er da Fornuften alene døbt,
ere Lidenskaberne Hedninger?

Young.

Kjøbenhavn 1843.

Faaes hos Universitetsboghandler C. A. Reitzel.

Trykt i Bianco Lunos Bogtrykkeri.

78 Kierkegaard *Enten-Eller* Copenhagen, 1843

80

Frederik Paludan-Müller (1809–1876) *Adam Homo, et Digt*

Copenhagen: C. A. Reitzel;
Bianco Luno,
1842–49

Paludan-Müller does for Danish poetry what Blicher does for Danish prose. He frees it from worn-out conventions and introduces new metrical forms. He is the first nineteenth-century poet to break away from the influence of Oehlenschläger, Ingemann, and Winther. His poetry is truly original.

Like Blicher, Paludan-Müller brings the realistic details of daily life to his poetry. He was born in a rather humble parsonage on the island of Fyn. His major character, Adam Homo, was born in a humble parsonage in Jutland. The language of *Adam Homo*, a satire in epic form, is infused with a bitter melancholy. Adam is a kind of Faust who leaves Jutland in search of worldly success in Copenhagen. He sacrifices love, goodness, and spiritual values for the recognition of society. Desolate, close to death, he is only saved by the grace of Alma, his true love.

Innovative and realistic, *Adam Homo* is also very much a philosophical poem. In his brooding search for salvation, Paludan-Müller is not unlike Kierkegaard. While criticizing bitterly the destructive material values of society, Paludan-Müller maintains hope that salvation is possible.

The first edition of *Adam Homo* is in three volumes, published in 1842 and 1849. When the first part was released in 1842, it was suppressed. Later it was revised and released in 1849 with parts two and three. On display here is the first part from 1842.

1968—Purchased with the William S. Spaulding Fund.

Georg Brandes and the "Modern Breakthrough"

Rahbek formed the major literary circle for the end of the eighteenth and beginning of the nineteenth century; Heiberg for the middle of the nineteenth; and Georg Brandes was the key critic for the end of the nineteenth and the beginning of the twentieth. Brandes lived a long life. He was born before Holger Drachmann, Jens Peter Jacobsen, and other modernists such as August Strindberg, and he outlived them all.

In the sixties, when he admonished Danish artists for being too complacent, for not keeping pace with Germany and France, Brandes was in turn roundly criticized. He had only a few followers. He left Copenhagen for several years and only returned in 1871 when he was promised a stipend and the opportunity to lecture freely at the University of Copenhagen.

As Steffens had been seventy years before, Brandes was a stirring lecturer. His lectures, which were published almost as soon they were given, fill a total of six volumes: *Hovedstrømninger i det nittende Aarhundredes Litteratur* (*Maincurrents in Nineteenth-Century Literature*). Brandes' essays sent shock waves through the literary world; nothing could be the same afterwards. Brandes inspired Danes to try the new Naturalism of France and Germany, to create a new literature which was closer to real life and which explored real social problems. He introduced Ibsen and other great modern writers to Denmark.

Holger Drachmann and Jens Peter Jacobsen are the most famous of the original Brandes circle. Drachmann dedicated his first collection of poetry to "My friend Dr. Georg Brandes" (81). Later, other Danes like Henrik Pontoppidan and Martin Andersen-Nexø joined the Brandes movement. Great writers outside as well as inside Denmark were stirred by the intellect of Georg Brandes. Ibsen was close to him, and Strindberg greatly admired his lectures. It was Brandes as much as Zola who inspired the Swedish playwright to write *Fadren* (*The Father*). Georg Brandes is truly an international Danish figure, a key inspiration in the "breakthrough of modern literature."

The second major collection of Brandes' critical essays is *Det moderne Gjennembruds Maend* (*The Men of the Modern Breakthrough*, 1883). Among the modernists Brandes discusses are Drachmann and Jacobsen.

81
Holger Drachmann (1846–1908) *Digte*

Copenhagen: Andr. Schou, [1872]

Drachmann was one of the first Danish poets to pick up the Brandes gauntlet. Having spent many months at sea with little to his name, working his way from port to port, Drachmann returned to Copenhagen in 1871, in time to hear the Brandes lectures. The combination of his contacts with radical free thinkers, his memories of suffering workers, and the inspiration of Brandes moved Drachmann to publish in 1872 this first collection of lyric poetry.

Drachmann had originally intended to make a living as a painter. His socialist convictions, however, compelled him to speak out against the oppression of the poor. Painting was not enough. Nevertheless, his sharp visual imagination and painterly moods inspired his poetry. His greatest lyrics paint pictures from the daily life of dockers and fishermen.

Holger Drachmann illustrated many of the title pages to his poetry collections. The title page for *Digte* is a wood engraving, signed "H.D."

1893—Purchased with the Lucy Osgood Fund.

82
Holger Drachmann (1846–1908)   *Sange ved Havet — Venezia*

Copenhagen: Gyldendal;
Thiele,
1877

As Blicher describes in prose the changing moods of the Jutland heaths, so does Drachmann in poetry capture the shifting moods of the sea. Some of his best lyric poetry is contained in this third collection. The illustrated title page is by Drachmann.

1893 — Purchased with the Lucy Osgood Fund.

83
Holger Drachmann (1846–1908)   *Troldtøj*

Copenhagen: Ernst Bojesen,
1889–90

Drachmann was also a writer of tales, in both poetry and prose. His shifting fantasies and impressionist moods were too expansive to limit him to one kind of writing. He never stayed in one place, restless and shifting from marriage to marriage, from radicalism to conservatism. Drachmann's writings not only describe the particulars of real life but also the inner life of a troubled, romantic soul.

Often he would draw upon Norse legend and folklore for inspiration. In this remarkable collage of poetry and prose, Drachmann creates a "folk saga for today." These visions of the "troll eye," illustrated with fantastic nightmare scenes, remind one of Edvard Munch or the later Strindberg.

This volume is open to an illustration from the "Mare" ("Nightmare") section. The credits for the artwork are listed on the title page as: "Joachim Skovgaard, Aug. Jerndorff, and Th. Bindesbøll." The photogravure illustrations are printed on tissue, tipped in.

1972 — Purchased with the Caroline Miller Parker Fund, in memory of Augustin H. Parker (HC 1897).

84
Jens Peter Jacobsen (1847–1885)   *Fru Marie Grubbe*

Copenhagen: Gyldendal (F. Hegel);
Graebe,
1876

Jacobsen is the most famous prose writer of the early Brandes circle. While Drachmann was tempestuous and troubled, Jacobsen was a steady ironist, recording the inevitable paradoxes of human life.

Jacobsen was trained as a biologist and in his early studies was deeply influenced by Darwin. He translated two key works by Darwin, and his first novel, *Mogens* (1872), demonstrates that human nature is controlled by environment and heredity. Jacobsen is the first writer of Danish Naturalist novels. Inspired by Brandes and the French novels of Flaubert, Stendahl, and Zola, Jacobsen wrote his second and most influential novel four years later, *Marie Grubbe, Interieurer fra det 17 Aarhundrede* (*Marie Grubbe, A Lady of the 17th Century*).

Fru Marie Grubbe is a historical novel, with the central character a high-born woman who lived in Jutland between 1643 and 1718. Having first married the son of a king, she ends up in poverty, the wife of a ferryman. Jacobsen shows that her destiny is inevitable, the result of her human nature and the circumstances in which she lived.

While writing *Marie Grubbe*, Jacobsen contracted tuberculosis. He never recovered and lived only another nine years. His other great novel *Niels Lyhne* was published in 1880.

1965 — Purchased with the George L. Lincoln (HC 1895) Fund.

85   Jacobsen   *Digte og Udkast*   Copenhagen, 1886

85
Jens Peter Jacobsen (1847–1885) *Digte og Udkast*

Copenhagen: Gyldendal
(F. Hegel & Son);
Bagge,
1886

Jacobsen is also a poet. But it was not until after his death when Edvard Brandes (Georg's brother) published this volume of poetry that Jacobsen became known as a poet.

Jacobsen uses medieval legend and ancient Norse motifs in a number of his poems. *Digte og Udkast* marks the first appearance in print of the famous *Gurresange*, a cycle of songs set to music by Arnold Schönberg in 1913.

The portrait frontispiece to this volume is an 1885 etching by Axel Helsted.

1960—Purchased with the Henry Wadsworth Longfellow Fund.

86
Georg Brandes (1842–1927) *Det Moderne Gjennembruds Maend*

Copenhagen: Gyldendal
(F. Hegel & Son);
Graebe,
1883

Jacobsen and Drachmann are among the group of writers Brandes introduces in this series of essays on writers of the "Modern Breakthrough." With his *Main Currents*, this collection of essays helped to create a new self-consciousness among those in the modernist movement.

Brandes' critical studies of other major authors such as Holberg, Kierkegaard, and Ibsen also mark him as one of the most influential critical voices of Scandinavian literature.

1927—Gift of Lucy W. Jennison.

87
Henrik Pontoppidan (1857–1943) *Lykke-Per*

Copenhagen: Nordiske Forlag;
Ernst Bojesen,
1898–1904

In 1917 Henrik Pontoppidan received international recognition when he shared the Nobel Prize for Literature. One of the most influential novelists in modern Scandinavia, Pontoppidan has been translated and widely studied.

A pessimist, ironist, realist, and satirist, he combines a number of late-nineteenth century influences. *Lykke Per* is one of his most famous novels and is a companion piece to the earlier *Det forjaetlede Land* (*The Promised Land*, 1881–95). The contrast between the idealist in *The Promised Land* and the self-centered Per is reminiscent of Ibsen's Brand-Peer Gynt poetic cycles. But Pontoppidan's Per is a creation of realistic fiction, a complex character full of contradictions. The Danish society which Pontoppidan satirizes is torn by modern paradoxes.

On display is the first volume, "Hans Ungdom" ("His Youth").

1929—Purchased with the Henry Wadsworth Longfellow Fund.

88
Johannes V. Jensen (1873–1950) *Myter og Jagter*

Copenhagen & Oslo:
Gyldendal;
Nordisk Forlag,
1907

With Pontoppidan, Jensen is a poet of the late nineteenth and early twentieth-century "modern breakthrough." With Pontoppidan (and Blicher), Jensen comes from Jutland. And like Pontoppidan, Jensen was awarded the Nobel Prize.

Jensen studied in Copenhagen, traveled to America and then to Spain. As a correspondent, he continued his travels throughout most of Europe. In his first great work, *Kongens Fald* (*Fall of the King*, 1900–01), Jensen creates his own original mythical style which has made him famous. He transforms his historical material, the story of Christian II, into a myth for modern Denmark.

After his second trip to America, Jensen wrote two more novels and the first of his celebrated *Myter* (*Myths*), a series of short prose pieces. The first collection was published in 1907; the last of a total of eleven volumes appeared in 1944. Jensen is as much a lyric poet as a prose artist. His myths are not limited by the particulars of realistic fiction but take on a universal, symbolic meaning.

On display here is the first *Myter* volume, with its original paper covers preserved.

1920—Purchased with the George Hayward, M.D. (HC 1809) Fund.

89
Martin Andersen-Nexø (1869–1954)   *Skygger*

Copenhagen: Jul. Gjellerup, 1898

Born into a poor working-class family in Copenhagen, Nexø first earned his living doing a variety of unskilled jobs. After studying to be a teacher, he worked as a journalist and free-lance writer. An avowed Communist, he spent most of his life in exile, including the Soviet Union and East Germany.

Nexø's first publication, *Skygger* (*Shadows*), is a series of short stories which depict the despair and oppression of poverty. These early stories are deeply pessimistic about the fate of the human race. But with his first major novel, *Pelle Erobreren* (*Pelle the Conquerer*, 1913–16), Nexø reveals his communist faith in the power of the working classes to change society. The later novels lose some of this optimism and are closer to the darker world of *Skygger*. But, despite his bitter attacks against the evils of society which cause human suffering, Nexø never takes away from his central characters their fundamental courage and human goodness which transcend oppression.

1986—Lent by the Boston Public Library.

MIN VEN

Dr. GEORG BRANDES

TILEGNET,

Isak Dinesen

Karen Blixen, or Isak Dinesen as she has come to be known, joins Pontoppidan, Jensen, and Nexø as the important innovators of twentieth-century Danish fiction. Through her father, Wilhelm Dinesen, she is a direct descendant of Georg Brandes' literary generation. But she belongs to no literary school. She is not particularly interested in social realism, in criticizing the social and political structures of Denmark and the world. Dinesen is highly personal and touches, rather, the universal soul of woman and man—the fantasies, the longing, the erotic, the dreams of love. She is gentle, tough, ironic, paradoxical; the richness of her prose is difficult to define. She resists all labels. Although her writing resonates with allusions to the past, Isak Dinesen always seems modern and highly original. In this sense, she inherits the Brandes spirit.

Other outstanding Danish writers could be chosen to join Dinesen as inheritors of Brandes' "modern breakthrough"—Martin A. Hansen, Kjeld Abell, Jacob Paludan, for example. Or Tom Kristensen, Tove Ditlevsen . . . the list goes on. Then there is the great Niels Bohr, who shares Dinesen's birth and death dates (1885–1962) and who ranks with Ørsted and Brahe as a world-famous scientist and writer of philosophical essays. He, too, deserves a place in this exhibition.

Yet, as a twentieth-century Danish literary artist of international significance, Isak Dinesen knows no equal. Even the Nobel laureates Jensen and Pontoppidan are not known as widely as Dinesen. It may be her American and African connections that broaden her appeal. Or perhaps it is that her writings are composed in English as well as in Danish, allowing her to reach more people more quickly, with her own voice rather than with the voice of a translator.

90
Wilhelm Dinesen (1845–1895)

Copenhagen: P. G. Philipsen;
Thiele,
1892

Nye Jagtbreve

Isak Dinesen's father, Wilhelm was a talented author. Recognized in the literary circles of Copenhagen, Wilhelm's writings are the subject of a Georg Brandes essay. Dinesen's major literary contributions are his two epistolary memoirs from America, *Jagtbreve* (1889) and *Nye Jagtbreve* (1892) (*Letters from the Hunt* and *New Letters from the Hunt*).

In publishing these *Letters*, Wilhelm Dinesen took the pseudonym Boganis which in Chippewa means hazelnut. He was given this name by the Indians during his hunting adventures in the Nebraska wilderness on his journey to America in the 1870s. He had felt close to the Indians and respected their sense of honor, their loyalty, courage, and reverence for nature.

Wilhelm's second daughter, Karen, was his favorite. There was a special bond between them, and any discussion of the influences on Isak Dinesen should include her father.

This first edition of *Nye Jagtbreve*, with its original paper covers, is illustrated by Erik Henningsen.

1986—Lent by Janet Jurist.

91
Isak Dinesen (1885–1962)   *Osceola*

Copenhagen:
Gyldendals Julebog,
1962

Several of Isak Dinesen's early stories and poems were not published until after her death in 1962. Her earliest work, a story called *Grjotgard Álvesøn og Aug* (*Grjotgard Álvesøn and Aug*), was written in 1905 when she was twenty. Isak's brother, Thomas Dinesen, preserved this story in its original manuscript form.

The editor, Clara Svendsen, gives this collection the title *Osceola*, a pseudonym Isak Dinesen had used for her early publications. Like her father, she chose an Indian name. Osceola was the proud leader of the Seminoles who, during the early nineteenth century, resisted the white intrusion into his Florida land and the attempts of the United States government to relocate him in Arkansas. Osceola was also the name Wilhelm Dinesen gave to his favorite dog.

Karen Dinesen Blixen published under a number of different pseudonyms. The name which she seemed finally to prefer and which emphasizes the link to her father is Isak Dinesen. "Isak" means in Hebrew "the one who laughs."

This copy is in the original covers and dust jacket.

1974—Gift of Robert D. Graff (HC 1941) and Mrs. Graff.

92
Isak Dinesen (1885–1962)   *Seven Gothic Tales*

New York:
Harrison Smith & Robert
Haas,
1934

Seven Gothic Tales, Dinesen's first important work and her first since returning from Africa in 1932, was written originally in English and published in the United States. She had trouble finding a publisher, and it was finally Robert Haas at Random House who agreed to risk the new and potentially controversial material. This edition, published in January 1934, was limited to 1010 copies. The Houghton copy is number 151. The illustrations for this limited edition are by Majeska.

Seven Gothic Tales was an immediate critical and commercial success and was reprinted in February by the Book-of-the-Month Club in a run of 50,000 copies.

1974—Gift of Robert D. Graff (HC 1941) and Mrs. Graff.

93
Isak Dinesen (1885–1962)   *Syv Fantastiske Fortaellinger*

Copenhagen: C. A. Reitzel,
1935

After returning from Kenya, Isak Dinesen settled down in her old family estate, Rungstedlund, fifteen miles north of Copenhagen. When *Seven Gothic Tales* was released in the United States, bringing this hitherto unknown Dane instant fame, Danish publishers rushed to locate the author and to obtain the rights for a Danish translation.

Dinesen finally sold these rights to Reitzel, an old publishing firm now owned by her brother-in-law, Knud Dahl. But when she saw samples of the translations being written for the Danish version, she decided to do her own. Rather than just allow a "translation," Dinesen reworked the text into Danish. But before she could complete this Danish version, her English text had been published in London and a Swedish translation in Stockholm.

The Danish version is shown here with its original decorated covers.

1966—Gift of James E. Walsh.

ISAK DINESEN

SYV

FANTASTISKE

FORTÆLLINGER

C.A.REITZELS FORLAG

93   Dinesen   *Syv Fantastiske Fortaellinger*   Copenhagen, 1935

94
Isak Dinesen (1885 – 1962)   *Den Afrikanske Farm*

Copenhagen: Gyldendal;
Nordisk Forlag;
1937

Dinesen's next major work, *Den afrikanske Farm* (*Out of Africa*), was also written first in English. But before submitting it for publication, she worked on the Danish version. It was her wish that the American, English, and Danish editions should all be published on the same day. Because of delays in releasing the proofs of the American version, the English and Danish editions were scheduled to appear before the American. Dinesen protested the change in schedule and tried to convince all three publishers to agree on one date. She was worried the delay would be seen as a slight to the American reading public, which had been so generous to her and had been the first to accept her work.

Her protests were to no avail: the Danish and the English appeared first. But the American public did not seem to mind. Her new book was accepted with even greater enthusiasm than *Seven Gothic Tales*.

In Denmark *Den afrikanske Farm* quickly became a favorite. Many preferred this moving autobiographical work to the earlier *Syv fantastiske Fortaellinger*, which had seemed strange and slightly decadent.

This copy is in the original decorated covers. A second copy, given to Houghton Library by Mr. and Mrs. Robert D. Graff, is inscribed by the author to Svend Borberg.

1986—Gift of James E. Walsh.

95
Isak Dinesen (1885 – 1962)   *Out of Africa*

London: Putnam,
1937

The first English-language version of *Den afrikanske Farm* appeared in London, a few weeks before the American edition. While perhaps a little more cautious, British reviews were also favorable.

1974—Gift of Robert D. Graff (HC 1941) and Mrs. Graff.

96
Isak Dinesen (1885 – 1962)   *Vinter-Eventyr*

Copenhagen: Gyldendal,
1942

The title of Dinesen's next work, *Vinter-Eventyr* (*Winter's Tales*, 1942), alludes to Shakespeare's play *The Winter's Tale*. These tales were written during the darkest days of the Nazi Occupation and a somber, winter mood prevails. Although they display some of the same sharp irony of the earlier allegorical *Gothic Tales*, the *Winter's Tales* seem more quietly resigned to the inevitable tragedies of life. Unlike the exotic world of *Gothic Tales*, the settings are closer to Dinesen's contemporary Scandinavia.

This copy is in the original paper covers.

1986—Gift of James E. Walsh.

97
Isak Dinesen (1885 – 1962)   *Winter's Tales*

New York: Random House,
1942

The American edition of Isak Dinesen's English version was published by Random House. This copy is in the original half blue cloth and dust jacket.

1974—Gift of Robert D. Graff (HC 1941) and Mrs. Graff.

94   Dinesen   *Den Afrikanske Farm*   Copenhagen, 1937

Abildgaard del: Clemens Sculps.